Gooseberry Patch

Harvest
Kitchen

T0028230

Gooseberry Patch

An imprint of Globe Pequot
64 South Main Street
Essex, CT 06426

www.gooseberrypatch.com

1•800•854•6673

Copyright 2023, Gooseberry Patch 978-1-62093-521-7
Photo Edition is a major revision of **Harvest Kitchen**.

Cover photo courtesy of **BeefItsWhatsforDinner.com**

Do you have a tried & true recipe...

tip, craft or memory that you'd like to see featured in
a **Gooseberry Patch** cookbook? Visit our website at
www.gooseberrypatch.com and follow the
easy steps to submit your favorite family recipe.

Or send them to us at:

Gooseberry Patch
PO Box 812
Columbus, OH 43216-0812

Don't forget to include the number of servings your recipe makes,
plus your name, address, phone number and email address. If we
select your recipe, your name will appear right along with it...
and you'll receive a **FREE** copy of the book!

Contents

Dedication

If you love the scent of apples ripe for picking, the glow of an autumn bonfire and the treats of Halloween...this book is for you.

Appreciation

A bushel of thanks for sending your best-of-the-best recipes to share this harvest season.

Classic
Casseroles
& Mains

Recipe for

On the MENU...

Copy and cut out this clever table tent. Fold it in half and jot down the recipe name...set it next to the food so everyone will know just what's for dinner!

On the MENU...

Crispy Pecan-Chicken Casserole

Michelle Greeley
Hayes, VA

Fast and fantastic!

2 c. cooked chicken, chopped
1/2 c. chopped pecans
1/8 c. onion, finely chopped
2 c. celery, sliced

1 c. mayonnaise
2 t. lemon juice
1 c. potato chips, crushed
1 c. shredded Cheddar cheese

Mix together all ingredients except chips and cheese. Place in a lightly greased 3-quart casserole dish. Combine chips and cheese; sprinkle on top. Bake, uncovered, at 375 degrees for 30 minutes. Serves 6.

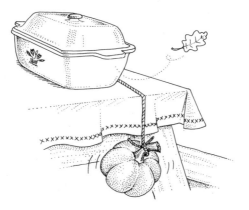

Autumn is a terrific time for a picnic. If it's a bit breezy, keep the tablecloth in place harvest-style. Place a length of jute down one long side and over the ends of the table. Tie the stem of a Jack-be-Little pumpkin to each end of the jute; repeat along the other side of the table. With the pumpkins hanging over the table's edge, the jute will keep the tablecloth just where you want it.

Biscuit & Beef Casserole

Shaynee Boynton
Las Vegas, NV

*My mom received this hearty recipe from her older sister
when I was just a baby.*

1 lb. ground beef, browned
   and drained
16-oz. can pork & beans
3/4 c. barbecue sauce
2 T. brown sugar, packed

1 T. dried, minced onion
1 t. salt
16.3-oz. tube refrigerated
   jumbo flaky biscuits, halved
1 c. shredded Cheddar cheese

Combine all ingredients except biscuits and cheese in a large saucepan over medium heat. Heat until bubbly; pour into a lightly greased 2-quart casserole dish. Place biscuits cut-side down around edge of casserole dish; sprinkle with cheese. Bake, uncovered, at 375 degrees for 20 to 30 minutes, until biscuits are golden. Serves 4 to 6.

A baked sweet potato is a fast-fix fall side for any main dish.
Simply bake until tender, then top with butter and
sprinkle with salt and paprika or a mixture of
cinnamon and sugar. Yum!

Classic Casseroles & Mains

Homestyle Shepherd's Pie

Barbara Nimmo-Tydings
Edgewater, MD

Our family's favorite and it only takes minutes to prepare. It's also a great dish for a large family...just double or triple the recipe.

1 lb. ground beef	4 to 5 c. mashed potatoes
1 onion, chopped	3/4 c. sour cream
10-3/4 oz. can tomato soup	1 c. shredded Cheddar cheese

Brown ground beef in a large skillet over medium heat. Add onion and cook until translucent; drain. Stir in soup; set aside. Combine potatoes and sour cream. In a greased 13"x9" baking pan, spread ground beef mixture, then potato mixture over top; sprinkle with cheese. Bake, uncovered, at 350 degrees for about 25 minutes, until cheese is golden and bubbly. Makes 6 to 8 servings.

We hail the merry harvest time,
the gayest of the year;
the time for rich and bounteous crops,
rejoicing and good cheer.

– Charles Dickens

Mexican Chicken Casserole

Michelle Townsend
Billings, MO

This has been an evolving dish for about the past five years. It can be adapted for those who love a little bit of zing, and for those who like a tamer side.

4 boneless, skinless chicken breasts, cooked and shredded
2 10-3/4 oz. cans cream of chicken soup
10-1/2 oz. can diced tomatoes with green chiles
1 T. pepper
1 T. fresh cilantro, chopped
2 cloves garlic, pressed
1 t. onion powder
1 t. cayenne pepper
8-oz. pkg. pasteurized process cheese spread, cubed
2 c. spicy nacho-flavored tortilla chips, crushed
Garnish: sour cream, sliced jalapeños, shredded lettuce, diced tomatoes

Combine all ingredients except tortilla chips and garnish. Mix well and pour into a lightly greased 13"x9" baking pan. Bake, uncovered, at 425 degrees for 20 minutes, or until bubbly. Stir well and top with crushed chips to cover. Bake for an additional 10 minutes. Let stand for 5 minutes before serving. Garnish as desired. Serves 6.

Bring armloads of late-blooming flowers, colorful leaves and bright berries indoors before the first frost. Tucked inside a vintage picnic tin or gathering basket, they're an autumn centerpiece in a snap.

Burgerito

Dori Cron
Paradise, CA

When my children and two nephews were teenagers, it seemed I was always cooking and looking for ways to make quick & easy, but great-tasting food. This is a recipe that I came up with one day when there was only one hour for dinner before evening events. The kids loved it and asked for it often.

1 sweet onion, chopped
2 15-oz. cans chili without
   beans
16-oz. can refried beans
16-oz. can chili beans

1 c. catsup
9-3/4 oz. pkg. corn chips
12-oz. pkg. shredded sharp
   Cheddar cheese

Sauté onion in a lightly greased skillet over medium heat until translucent. Mix together remaining ingredients except cheese; spread in a lightly greased 13"x9" baking pan. Top with cheese and bake, uncovered, at 350 degrees for about 20 minutes, until cheese is bubbly. Serves 8 to 10.

What a clever placecard! Pull back the husks on ears of mini Indian corn and use a bronze or gold paint pen to write the name of each guest along the husks. Arrange one ear of corn in the center of each plate.

Ham & Pineapple Dinner

Stephanie Mayer
Portsmouth, VA

A great-tasting dinner and a quick-fix anytime.

2 T. butter
2-1/2 c. cooked ham, cubed
2 green onions, chopped
1 c. pineapple chunks, drained
1-1/3 c. pineapple juice

4 t. cider vinegar
2 T. brown sugar, packed
2 t. mustard
2 T. cornstarch

Melt butter in a large skillet over medium heat. Sauté ham, onions and pineapple for about 5 minutes. Combine remaining ingredients in a small bowl. Stir together well and pour over mixture in skillet. Mix well; cook until thickened and heated through, about 5 minutes. Serves 4.

Create a homespun welcome...fill an old-fashioned wooden wheelbarrow with pumpkins, gourds and bittersweet. Add some unexpected colors by tucking in a few green pumpkins along with some white ones...how fun!

Potato & Sausage Casserole

Lori Gartzke
Fargo, ND

This casserole is one of our family's favorites. My husband jokingly says that if I ever leave him, I have to give him the recipe! Easily doubled or tripled for a potluck dish if you have a large roaster. My mom used to make it for our family reunion every year, and even though she is gone now, my sisters and I try to make sure one of us still makes it. We never have any leftovers!

1 lb. ground seasoned pork
    sausage
1 onion, chopped
5 potatoes, peeled and sliced

10-3/4 oz. can cream of
    mushroom soup
2 to 3 c. milk
salt and pepper to taste

Brown sausage and onion in a large skillet over medium heat; drain. Arrange potatoes in a Dutch oven; top with sausage mixture. Stir together soup and 2 cups milk; pour over potato mixture. If needed, add additional milk to almost cover potatoes. Sprinkle with salt and pepper. Bake, uncovered, at 350 degrees for one to 1-1/2 hours, until potatoes are tender. This can also be simmered on the stove if you have a large skillet, for about 30 minutes, or until potatoes are tender. Serves 6.

Company coming? Put flannel sheets and wool blankets on the beds to warm up the chilly nights...oh-so cozy!

Pork Chop & Wild Rice Casserole

Mary Drummond
Clarkson, NE

I enjoy making this with leftover pork chops.

6 pork chops, cooked
1 c. wild rice, cooked
1 onion, chopped
1 green pepper, chopped

6 mushrooms, chopped
1/2 t. salt
1/4 t. pepper
2 c. beef or chicken broth

Place pork chops in a greased 2-1/2 quart casserole dish. Spoon rice over chops. Add onion and green pepper; sprinkle with salt and pepper. Pour broth over top. Cover and bake at 350 degrees for 30 minutes. If too moist, remove cover and bake until moisture evaporates. Serves 4 to 6.

Place a pretty pressed leaf on each folded napkin,
then tie on a length of pumpkin-colored ribbon.

Creamy Chicken Casserole

Stepheny Milo
Sacramento, CA

This is the best chicken casserole...everyone will love it! The secret is to make a perfect sauce, take your time and it will turn out really good. You'll win a blue ribbon!

2/3 c. oil
1/2 c. all-purpose flour
1/4 to 1/2 c. chili powder
1/2 t. dried oregano
1/4 t. salt
3 cloves garlic, finely chopped
6 c. chicken broth
4 c. cooked chicken breasts, diced
1 c. sour cream

5 c. shredded Monterey Jack cheese, divided
Optional: 2 8-3/4 oz. cans corn, drained
Optional: 1 carrot, peeled and shredded
12 6-inch corn tortillas, cut into bite-size pieces
Optional: 3.8-oz. can chopped black olives, drained

Heat oil in a large skillet over medium-low heat. Add flour, seasonings and garlic; cook for 5 to 7 minutes. Add broth; simmer until thickened, about 30 minutes. In a large bowl, combine chicken, sour cream, 2 cups cheese, corn and carrots, if using; mix well. In a greased 13"x9" baking pan, spoon half the sauce, tortilla pieces and chicken mixture; repeat layers. Sprinkle with remaining shredded cheese and olives, if desired. Cover with aluminum foil and bake for 30 minutes at 350 degrees. Remove foil and bake for an additional 5 minutes. Serves 6.

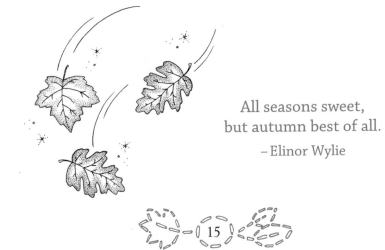

All seasons sweet,
but autumn best of all.

– Elinor Wylie

Pizza Casserole

Holly Davis
Newnan, GA

*For a make-ahead meal, cover the extra casserole and freeze for up to
3 months. To bake the frozen casserole, thaw it in the refrigerator
overnight and bake at 350 degrees for 35 to 40 minutes, until hot.*

2 lbs. ground beef
1 onion, chopped
2 28-oz. jars spaghetti sauce
16-oz. pkg. spiral pasta, cooked

2 8-oz. pkgs. shredded
  mozzarella cheese
8-oz. pkg. sliced pepperoni

In a large skillet over medium heat, brown beef and onion; drain. Stir
in spaghetti sauce and pasta. Transfer to 2 greased, 13"x9" baking
pans. Sprinkle with cheese; top with pepperoni. Bake, uncovered,
at 350 degrees for 25 to 30 minutes. Makes 2 pans; each pan
serves 8 to 10.

Fill an egg basket or enamelware pail to overflowing with
red, yellow and green apples...a whimsical fall touch
for the porch or by the fireplace.

Joe's Favorite Pasta

Rebecca Aikens
Clarion, PA

This is my husband's favorite pasta dish. A recipe I've tweaked from other recipes, it's a big hit in our home!

1 bulb garlic
1/4 c. plus 2 t. olive oil, divided
14-1/2 oz. can diced tomatoes
2 to 3 t. dried basil
1/4 to 1/2 t. red pepper flakes
salt to taste
16-oz. pkg. linguine pasta,
   uncooked

Slice 1/4 inch off top of garlic bulb; drizzle with 2 teaspoons olive oil. Wrap in aluminum foil; bake at 350 degrees for 25 minutes. Remove garlic from oven; let stand. In a large bowl, combine tomatoes and seasonings; mix well. Remove garlic from aluminum foil and squeeze out cloves; chop finely and add to tomato mixture. Refrigerate for at least 2 hours. When ready to serve, cook pasta according to package directions; drain. Combine hot pasta with cold tomato sauce; mix well. Serves 6.

Twine fresh bittersweet vines around & around and you've created a wreath in no time. Just secure the ends with a bit of wire, make a wire loop and hang on a picket gate.

Chicken & Dressing Casserole

Tracie Loyd
Powell, TN

Great for any gathering!

1/2 c. margarine
1 c. celery, chopped
1 c. onion, chopped
2 c. cornbread crumbs
2 c. bread crumbs
dried sage to taste

10-3/4 oz. can cream of
  chicken soup
Optional: 1/4 to 1/2 c. water
5 boneless, skinless chicken
  breasts, cooked and diced
10-1/2 oz. jar chicken gravy

Heat margarine in a large skillet over medium heat. Add celery and onion; cook until tender. Combine celery mixture, cornbread crumbs, bread crumbs, sage and soup. If desired, add water to reach desired consistency. Transfer to a lightly greased 13"X9" baking pan. Arrange chicken over top; spread gravy over chicken. Bake, covered, at 375 degrees for one hour. Serves 12.

An antique wire basket makes a great container for holding jars of jams & jellies and fruits & veggies found at roadside farmstands during harvest time. Once the basket is back home, fill it with pumpkins of all sizes and colors.

Baked Mushroom Chicken

Nancy Girard
Chesapeake, VA

Pure comfort food. I always add a few more mushrooms because I love them.

4 boneless, skinless chicken
   breasts
1/4 c. all-purpose flour
3 T. butter
1 c. sliced mushrooms
1/2 c. chicken broth

1/4 t. salt
1/8 t. pepper
1/3 c. shredded mozzarella
   cheese
1/3 c. grated Parmesan cheese
1/4 c. green onions, sliced

With a rolling pin or mallet, flatten chicken to 1/2-inch thick. Combine chicken and flour in a large plastic zipping bag; shake to coat evenly. Melt butter in a large skillet and brown chicken, about 2 minutes per side. Arrange chicken in a greased 13"x9" baking pan. Sauté mushrooms in same skillet until tender. Add broth, salt and pepper to skillet. Bring to a boil for 5 minutes; reduce liquid by about half. Spoon over chicken. Bake, uncovered, at 375 degrees for 15 minutes. Sprinkle with cheeses and top with onions; return to oven. Bake for an additional 5 minutes, until cheese is melted. Serves 4.

This season, try tucking candles into unexpected containers.
Mason jars filled with birdseed hold taper candles
in place, while custard cups filled with water
are ideal for floating candles.

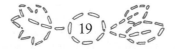

Lazy Day Casserole

Judy Gates
Elberfeld, IN

You'll love the flavor of this casserole.

2 onions, chopped
1-1/2 c. celery, diced
1 T. oil
1 lb. ground beef
1/2 c. long-cooking rice, uncooked

10-3/4 oz. can cream of chicken soup
10-3/4 oz. can cream of mushroom soup
5-oz. can chow mein noodles

In a skillet over medium heat, sauté onions and celery in oil; set aside. Add ground beef to skillet. Cook until no longer pink; drain. Add onion mixture, rice and soups; mix well. Pour into a lightly greased 2-quart casserole dish. Cover and bake at 400 degrees for 35 minutes. Sprinkle noodles evenly over casserole. Bake, uncovered, for an additional 10 minutes. Serves 6.

So clever...store summer's small gardening tools with the help of an old metal rake head. Just mount it upside-down on the potting shed wall.

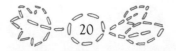

Ham & Potato Scallop

Janet Williams
Santa Ana, CA

*This is always one of the first dishes to go, no leftovers here! I take
copies of the recipe with me just in case someone asks.*

3 T. butter
1/4 c. onion, grated
1/4 c. green pepper, chopped
3 T. all-purpose flour
1 t. salt
1/8 t. pepper
1/2 t. dry mustard

1-1/2 c. milk
1 c. shredded sharp Cheddar
  cheese, divided
5 to 6 potatoes, peeled
  and sliced
1-1/2 c. cooked ham, diced

Melt butter in a large skillet over medium heat. Add onion and green
pepper; cook until tender. Blend in flour and seasonings. Gradually
add milk; stir until thickened. Blend in 3/4 cup cheese. Layer sliced
potatoes, ham and sauce alternately in a greased 2-1/2 quart casserole
dish. Cover and bake at 350 degrees for one hour. Uncover; sprinkle
with remaining cheese. Bake, uncovered, for an additional 15 minutes,
or until potatoes are tender. Serves 4 to 6.

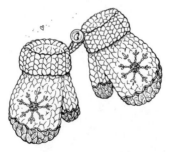

When the weather gets brisk, it's time to pull out the
warm, woolly mittens...but they can easily get separated
from each other. Keep them together by stitching a button
to the underside of one mitten, then stitch a loop of
embroidery floss to the inside of the other. Simply fasten
together after taking them off!

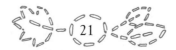

Theresa's Spaghetti Casserole

Theresa Wehmeyer
Rosebud, MO

Have you ever lost a treasured recipe? Well, that's the story with this recipe. I searched and searched for years thinking I had lost it. Imagine my shock, when going through my unorganized recipe box, at finding this long-lost family favorite...I felt like a dog finding a buried bone!

2 T. margarine
1/2 c. green onions, sliced
1/2 c. celery, sliced
4-oz. can sliced mushrooms, drained
8-oz. pkg. shredded Monterey Jack cheese, divided
8-oz. pkg. spaghetti, cooked
3 c. cooked ham, cubed
1 c. sour cream
1 c. cottage cheese
1 c. frozen green beans, thawed
1/4 t. garlic salt
1/8 t. pepper

Melt margarine in a large skillet over medium heat. Add onions, celery and mushrooms; cook until tender. Remove from heat; combine with 1-1/2 cups cheese and remaining ingredients. Transfer to a greased 2-quart casserole dish. Bake, covered, at 350 degrees for 20 minutes. Sprinkle with remaining cheese. Bake for an additional 10 minutes, until cheese is bubbly and melted. Serves 8.

A new twist on Jack-'O-Lanterns...use a small bit to drill holes into dried gourds. Insert a bulb or two from a string of low-voltage lights into each, then arrange the gourds in a bowl or along a mantel. It's easy to hide the light's cord...just cover with fall leaves.

Classic Casseroles & Mains

Mrs. Wrestlake's Goulash

Kathleen Walker
Mountain Center, CA

When my grandmother would come to visit, I remember the delicious smells wafting through the house while she was cooking. My mother and she cooked together often, including Christmas cookies, baking days throughout the year, and, of course, this delicious recipe of which she was so proud. I always looked forward to her arrival.

2 T. butter
1-1/2 lbs. beef chuck roast, cubed
2 t. salt
1 t. pepper
2 t. paprika
1 onion, finely chopped

2 cloves garlic, finely chopped
2 T. all-purpose flour
1 c. tomato purée
2 c. beef broth
2 c. potatoes, peeled and cubed
cooked wide egg noodles
1/4 c. butter, melted

Melt butter in a stockpot over medium heat; add beef and brown on all sides. Sprinkle with salt, pepper and paprika; stir in onion and garlic. Cook until onion begins to soften. Stir in flour until smooth; add tomato purée and broth. Cover and simmer, stirring occasionally, for about 45 minutes. Add potatoes; cover and continue to cook until potatoes are done, about 45 minutes. Toss noodles and melted butter together; serve goulash spooned over noodles. Serves 8.

Greet family & friends with apple photo frames! Glue a small clip clothespin to the end of a short stick; let dry. Push the opposite end of the stick into a shiny apple, then clip a favorite photo onto the clothespin.

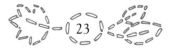

Chicken & Broccoli Puffs

Tasha Petenzi
Goodlettsville, TN

This recipe is a super easy, cheesy favorite.

10-oz. tube refrigerated
   crescent rolls
2 10-oz. cans chicken, drained
10-3/4 oz. can cream of
   chicken soup

1 c. milk
8-oz. pkg. shredded Cheddar
   cheese
10-oz. pkg. frozen chopped
   broccoli, cooked and drained

Separate crescent rolls; place one tablespoon chicken in the center of each. Roll up according to package directions. Arrange rolls in a lightly greased 13"x9" baking pan. Mix together soup, milk and cheese; pour over crescent rolls. Bake, uncovered, at 350 degrees for approximately one hour, or until rolls are golden. Spoon cheese sauce from chicken puffs over broccoli and serve together. Serves 4.

Fresh, green salads are the perfect go-along with casseroles.
Keep it oh-so easy by picking up a bag of fresh spinach and
tossing with toasted pecans and dried cranberries or apricots.
Top with a splash of balsamic vinegar dressing...mmm!

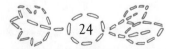

Mom's Chicken Pot Pie

Wyndi Sanchez
Orange Grove, TX

Growing up, this was my favorite recipe...something special that my mom would make just for me. Mom is no longer with us, but whenever I make this recipe, I think of her...I share it in loving memory of Cathy Hanzelka.

3 to 4-lb. chicken
10-3/4 oz. can cream of
　chicken soup
10-3/4 oz. can cream of
　celery soup
16-oz. pkg. frozen mixed
　vegetables

salt, pepper and garlic powder
　to taste
1 c. all-purpose flour
1 c. milk
1/2 c. butter, melted

Cover chicken with water in a stockpot. Simmer over medium heat until chicken is tender, about one to 1-1/2 hours. Remove chicken, reserving broth. Let cool; remove and discard skin and bones. Shred chicken. Mix together chicken, soups, one cup reserved broth and vegetables in a greased 13"x9" baking pan. Sprinkle with salt, pepper and garlic powder. For crust, stir together flour, milk and butter until smooth; spread over chicken mixture. Bake, uncovered, at 350 degrees for 45 minutes to one hour, until crust is golden. Makes 6 to 8 servings.

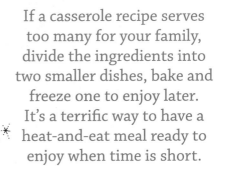

If a casserole recipe serves too many for your family, divide the ingredients into two smaller dishes, bake and freeze one to enjoy later. It's a terrific way to have a heat-and-eat meal ready to enjoy when time is short.

Aunt Barb's Veggie Casserole

Samantha Moyer
Farragut, IA

This is my favorite holiday casserole. The recipe was given to my mom years ago, and it's been on our holiday table ever since.

16-oz. pkg. frozen chopped
   broccoli, cooked and drained
16-oz. pkg. frozen cauliflower,
   cooked and drained
8-oz. pkg. pasteurized process
   cheese spread, sliced

2 sleeves round buttery
   crackers, crushed
1 c. margarine, melted

Spread cooked vegetables in a greased 13"x9" baking pan; layer with cheese. Top with cracker crumbs; drizzle with melted margarine. Bake, uncovered, at 350 degrees for 30 to 40 minutes. Makes 6 to 8 servings.

Everyone must take time to sit and watch the leaves turn.

– Elizabeth Lawrence

Party Potatoes

Margaret Bousman
Riverside, CA

This is an all-time favorite for the teachers and staff at the school where I teach. Don't blink, because it is gone in an instant! To make it even heartier, you can add cooked chicken and broccoli.

1/4 c. butter, melted
30-oz. pkg. frozen cubed
   hashbrowns, thawed
10-3/4 oz. cream of
   chicken soup

8-oz. pkg. shredded Cheddar
   cheese
16-oz. container sour cream

Pour butter into a 13"x9" baking pan; spread hashbrowns in pan. Heat undiluted soup in a saucepan over medium heat; gradually add cheese, stirring constantly until melted. Add sour cream to soup mixture; stir until well mixed. Pour over hashbrowns and mix gently. Lightly pat mixture into an even layer. Bake, uncovered, at 350 degrees for about 45 minutes. Serves 6 to 8.

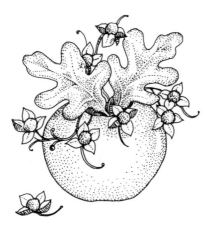

Turn a hollowed-out apple into a mini vase...fill it with water, then add fresh leaves and bittersweet berries.

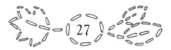

Cordon Bleu Casserole

Shirley McGlin
Black Creek, WI

Elegant, but so easy to make...sure to become a new favorite.

8 boneless, skinless chicken
  breasts
1/2 to 3/4 lb. deli shaved ham
  or dried beef
1 c. sliced mushrooms
8 slices Swiss cheese, divided

10-3/4 oz. can cream of
  chicken soup
1/4 c. water
3 c. bread cubes
1/2 c. butter, melted

Arrange chicken in a lightly greased 13"x9" baking pan. Layer ingredients over chicken in following order: ham or dried beef, mushrooms and cheese. Mix soup with water and pour over top. Toss bread cubes with butter; spoon over casserole. Bake, uncovered, for 1-1/2 hours at 325 degrees. Serves 6 to 8.

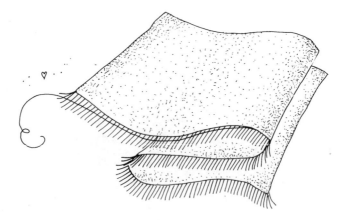

A cut-to-size length of linen or medium-weave burlap makes a great no-sew tablecloth. To add fringe, just pull away threads, one row at a time.

Classic Casseroles & Mains

He-Man Casserole

Linda Barner
Fresno, CA

This recipe was published in my church cookbook in 1983. So hearty, filled with ham and mashed potatoes...that must be how it got its name!

6 T. butter
1/2 c. onion, chopped
1/2 c. green pepper, chopped
6 T. all-purpose flour
1/8 t. pepper
1-1/2 c. milk
1 c. chicken broth

4 c. cooked ham, cubed
10-oz. pkg. frozen peas, thawed
    and drained
4 c. mashed potatoes
1 egg, beaten
1 c. shredded Cheddar cheese

Melt butter in a large skillet over medium heat. Add onion and green pepper; sauté until tender. Add flour and pepper; stir until smooth. Gradually stir in milk and broth. Cook, stirring until thickened. Stir in ham and peas; pour into a lightly greased 3-quart casserole dish. In a large bowl, combine mashed potatoes, egg and cheese. Drop by spoonfuls onto ham mixture. Bake, uncovered, at 375 degrees for 45 minutes, or until hot and bubbly. Serves 8.

Welcome friends & family to the table with words from the heart. A fabric marker in gold, copper or bronze is perfect for adding names to napkins or writing words of thanks along a table runner or tablecloth edge.

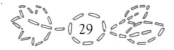

Potatoes, Sausage & Peppers

Jackie Flood
Geneseo, NY

*My mom gave me this recipe a year ago...I tried it and loved it!
I made it last night and tweaked it a bit to make it more like a stew.
I stirred together the optional flour and water to make a paste, then
blended it into the skillet.*

1 T. olive oil
3 Italian sausage links
1 green pepper, sliced
1 red pepper, sliced
1-1/3 c. water
1.35-oz. pkg. onion soup mix

3 potatoes, baked, peeled
  and cubed
salt and pepper to taste
Optional: 2 T. all-purpose flour,
  1/4 c. water

Heat oil in a large skillet over medium heat; add sausage and brown.
Remove sausage and set aside, reserving drippings in skillet. Add
peppers to reserved drippings; sauté for 5 minutes, or until they begin
to soften. Stir in water, soup mix and potatoes. Bring to a boil. Cover;
simmer for 10 to 15 minutes, until potatoes are heated through and
tender. Serve with sausage links. Serves 4.

Keep an eye open at tag sales for a wicker backpack.
Filled to the brim with fall foliage, it makes a welcome
back-door greeting.

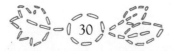

Easy Chicken & Mushrooms

Jennifer Levy
Warners, NY

I made up this recipe on a cold winter's night after going "shopping" in my pantry. It's quick, easy and very yummy! The sauce is delicious with mashed potatoes. My husband and kids love it!

4 boneless, skinless
   chicken breasts
salt and pepper to taste
2 T. olive oil
1 t. garlic, minced
10-3/4 oz. can golden
   mushroom soup

1/2 c. dry white wine or
   chicken broth
1/2 c. water
1/4 c. Kalamata olives, pitted
   and sliced
2 t. lemon juice
2 T. fresh parsley, chopped

With a mallet, pound chicken to 1/4-inch thick; sprinkle with salt and pepper. Heat oil in a large skillet over medium heat. Brown chicken on both sides, about 4 minutes per side. Remove chicken; set aside. Add garlic, soup, wine or broth, water, olives and lemon juice to skillet; stir up browned bits. Bring to a simmer; cook for 2 minutes. Add chicken and parsley; heat through. Serves 4.

Keep plenty of apples on hand (towels too!) to enjoy an old-fashioned game of bobbing for apples. Make it easy for little ones by leaving the stems on the apples.

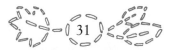

Crescent-Topped Chicken

Beth Shaeffer
Greenwood, IN

This is always a quick & easy meal to get on the table after a busy day. With meat, veggies and bread all in one casserole, all you need to add is a crisp green salad.

16-oz. pkg. frozen broccoli,
 cauliflower & carrot blend,
 thawed and drained
2 c. cooked chicken, cubed
10-3/4 oz. can cream of
 potato soup

1 c. milk
3/4 c. shredded Cheddar cheese
3/4 c. French fried onions
1/2 t. seasoned salt
2 8-oz. tubes refrigerated
 crescent rolls

Combine all ingredients except rolls; pour into a greased 13"x9" baking pan. Bake, uncovered, at 350 degrees for 30 minutes. Unroll crescent rolls and separate into triangles. Arrange triangles over casserole, overlapping a little if necessary. Return to oven; bake for an additional 15 to 20 minutes, until crust is golden. Makes 6 to 8 servings.

How about a game of pumpkin bowling? Pumpkins can be rolled toward 2-liter bottles filled with water, and depending on the ages of the kids, they can stand closer or farther away from the pins.

Company's Coming Casserole

Kim Runyon
Carlisle, OH

Mom used to make this dish when I was a little girl. Through the years the recipe was misplaced, then three years ago it was found in her cupboard under the shelf paper!

2 to 3 T. oil
6 chicken breasts
1 t. salt
1/4 t. pepper
10-3/4 oz. can cream of
   chicken soup
3/4 c. white wine or
   chicken broth

4-oz. can mushroom stems and
   pieces, drained
8-oz. can sliced water chestnuts,
   drained
2 T. green pepper, chopped
1/4 t. dried thyme
cooked rice

Heat oil in a large skillet over medium heat. Sprinkle chicken with salt and pepper; add to skillet and cook until lightly golden on both sides. Remove chicken from skillet, reserving drippings. Place chicken skin-side up in a lightly greased 11"x7" baking pan. Stir soup into reserved drippings; gradually stir in wine or broth. Add mushrooms, water chestnuts, green pepper and thyme; bring to a boil over medium heat. Pour around chicken. Bake, covered, at 350 degrees for 25 minutes; uncover and bake for an additional 25 to 30 minutes, until chicken is tender. Serve with rice. Makes 6 servings.

Hollow out a speckled turban squash and fill with a favorite dip for veggies or chips...a fall twist on a serving bowl!

Chicken & Biscuit Pie

Shell Bueche
Ames, IA

My aunt taught me to make this dish during our annual family summer vacation. Now I make it whenever I need to make a dinner dish for church or school potlucks...the casserole dish is always empty by the time we leave.

10-3/4 oz. cream of
   chicken soup
2/3 c. mayonnaise
2 to 3 t. Worcestershire sauce
4 c. cooked chicken, cubed
3 c. broccoli, chopped
Optional: 1 onion, chopped
8-oz. pkg. shredded Cheddar-
   Jack cheese

4 7-1/2-oz. tubes refrigerated
   buttermilk biscuits, halved
1 egg, beaten
1/3 c. sour cream
1 t. celery seed
1/2 t. salt
Optional: 1 t. celery flakes

Combine soup, mayonnaise and Worcestershire sauce in a bowl. Stir in chicken, broccoli and onion, if using. Transfer to 2 greased, 13"x9" baking pans; sprinkle with cheese. Cover and bake at 375 degrees for 20 minutes. Arrange biscuit halves over hot chicken mixture. Combine remaining ingredients in a bowl; pour over biscuits. Bake, uncovered, for an additional 20 minutes, or until golden. Makes 2 pans; each pan serves 8 to 10.

The next time you pop popcorn, sprinkle in a bit of sugar to taste...super-simple kettle corn!

for a poppin' good time!

Tuna Penne Casserole

Jackie Flood
Geneseo, NY

I have made this recipe over and over again. It's an amazing recipe...
so different from the tuna noodle casserole I grew up with.

1/4 lb. sliced mushrooms
1 green onion, minced
2 T. fresh Italian parsley, minced
6-oz. can tuna, drained
1-1/8 c. whole-wheat penne
   pasta, cooked

1/2 c. sour cream
1/4 c. mayonnaise
1 t. Dijon mustard
Optional: 1 T. dry white wine
1/4 c. shredded Cheddar cheese

Spray a skillet with non-stick vegetable spray. Add mushrooms, onion
and parsley; sauté over medium heat. Add tuna; simmer until heated
through. Stir tuna mixture into drained pasta; blend in sour cream,
mayonnaise, mustard and wine, if using. Pour into a lightly greased
2-quart casserole dish; sprinkle top with cheese. Bake, uncovered, at
375 degrees for 30 minutes. Serves 2.

Placed on a simple ironstone plate, pears make an easy,
natural centerpiece. Try using Bosc, Green Anjou and
Red Bartlett for a little autumn color.

Tuscan Pork Loin

Gina McClenning
Valrico, FL

A delicious pork loin for holiday gatherings. Guests always ask for this recipe and leftovers are delicious the next day. Sometime, instead of cream cheese, try garlic and herb spreadable cheese.

4-lb. boneless pork loin roast
8-oz. pkg. cream cheese, softened
1 T. dried pesto seasoning
1/2 c. baby spinach
6 slices bacon, crisply cooked

12-oz. jar roasted red peppers, drained and divided
1 t. paprika
1 t. salt
1/2 t. pepper
Garnish: baby spinach

Slice pork lengthwise, cutting down center, but not through other side. Open halves and cut down center of each half, cutting to, but not through other sides. Open into a rectangle. Place plastic wrap over pork and pound to an even thickness with a meat mallet or rolling pin. Spread cream cheese evenly over pork. Sprinkle with pesto seasoning; arrange spinach over cream cheese. Top with bacon and half the red peppers, reserving remaining peppers for another recipe. Roll up pork lengthwise; tie at 2-inch intervals with kitchen string. Rub pork with paprika, salt and pepper. Place seam-side down on a lightly greased rack on an aluminum foil-lined baking sheet. Bake at 425 degrees for 30 minutes, or until a meat thermometer inserted into thickest portion registers 155 degrees. Remove from oven; let stand for 10 minutes. Remove string from pork; slice 1/2-inch thick. Serve pork slices on a bed of spinach leaves. Serves 8 to 10.

An apple, mini pumpkin or pear makes a clever napkin weight when dinner goes outside for an autumn picnic.

Slowly-
Simmered
Suppers

Autumn is for Planting

Bulbs that are planted in crisp autumn weather, such as tulips, daffodils, crocus and hyacinths will flower next spring. From February through June your garden will be in full bloom!

Here's how to get started...

Spring blooming bulbs need to go into the ground before the ground freezes...a warm fall day is ideal.

Plant bulbs in a sunny location. The only exceptions are crocus, daffodils and hyacinths which will bloom in part shade.

How deep to plant bulbs depends on the bulb... be sure to read the packaging to learn the proper planting distance for a particular variety. As a general rule of thumb, the hole should be 3 times as deep as the size of the bulb.

Easy as 1...2...3...4!

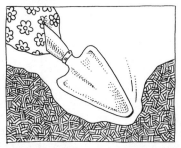

1. Dig a hole to the proper depth

2. Place the bulb in the hole

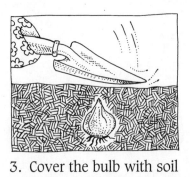

3. Cover the bulb with soil

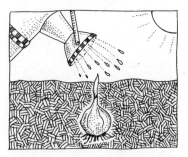

4. Water thoroughly

Slowly-Simmered *Suppers*

Pork Roast with Garlic & Apples

Annette Ingram
Grand Rapids, MI

Last summer our family traveled to a bed & breakfast in the quaint town of Niagara-on-the-Lake in Canada. This delicious pork roast was served the first night...I'm so glad the innkeeper shared this recipe with me!

4-lb. boneless pork loin roast,
    halved
12-oz. jar apple jelly
1/2 c. water

2-1/2 t. garlic, minced
1 T. dried parsley
1 t. seasoned salt
1 t. pepper

Place roast in a slow cooker. Whisk together jelly, water and garlic; pour over roast. Sprinkle with seasonings. Cover and cook on low setting for 8 to 9 hours, or until a meat thermometer inserted in thickest part of roast reads 160 degrees. Let stand for 5 minutes before slicing. Serve with cooking juices, if desired. Serves 12.

Slow cookers come in all sizes, so why not have a couple on hand? A large-size slow cooker is ideal for family-size roasts or turkey breasts, while a smaller size is just right for a savory appetizer dip or fondue.

Nancy's Winter Stew

Nancy Fagan
Warminster, PA

A great recipe for warming up on the coldest days!

10-3/4 oz. can tomato soup
1/4 c. dry red wine or beef broth
1-1/3 c. water
1/2 c. onion, chopped
1/4 t. Italian seasoning
salt and pepper to taste

2 to 3 potatoes, peeled and cubed
2 carrots, peeled and sliced
 1/2-inch thick
14-1/2 oz. can green beans,
 drained
1 doz. frozen meatballs

Mix together soup, wine or broth and water in a slow cooker. Stir in remaining ingredients. Cover and cook on low setting for 8 to 9 hours. Makes 4 servings.

Smokey White Bean Chili

Lorrie Smith
Drummonds, TN

I love white bean chili, but don't care for the chicken, so I decided to try it with smoked sausages. Now I wouldn't make it any other way!

5 15-1/2 oz. cans Great
 Northern beans, drained
 and rinsed
16-oz. pkg. mini smoked
 sausages

10-oz. can diced tomatoes with
 green chiles
1 T. dried, minced onion
1 T. chili powder
salt and pepper to taste

Combine all ingredients in a slow cooker. Cover and cook on low setting for about 4 hours. Makes 6 to 8 servings.

Don't peek...lifting the lid will increase a slow cooker's cooking time.

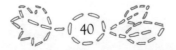

Best-Ever Lasagna

Cherylann Smith
Efland, NC

This is a quick, easy recipe for homestyle lasagna. Great with garlic bread and salad.

1 lb. ground beef, browned and drained	1/3 c. water
1 t. Italian seasoning	Optional: 4-oz. can sliced mushrooms, drained
8 lasagna noodles, uncooked and broken into thirds	15-oz. container ricotta cheese
28-oz. jar spaghetti sauce	8-oz. pkg. shredded mozzarella cheese

Combine ground beef and Italian seasoning. Arrange half the lasagna noodles in a greased slow cooker. Spread half the ground beef mixture over noodles. Top with half each of remaining ingredients. Repeat layering process. Cover and cook on low setting for 5 hours. Serves 10.

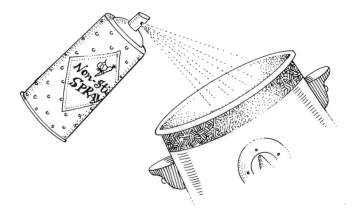

Slow cooking is so easy, keep clean-up a snap too...just spray the inside of the crock with non-stick vegetable spray before adding any ingredients. You can even pick up a handy slow-cooker liner...just toss when it's time to clean up!

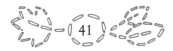

French Onion Soup

Robin Hill
Rochester, NY

*Now you can enjoy this elegant soup any time
and it's so easy to prepare.*

1/4 c. butter	1/4 c. dry white wine or
3 c. onion, sliced	beef broth
1 T. sugar	6 slices French bread
1 t. salt	1/2 c. grated Parmesan cheese
2 T. all-purpose flour	1/2 c. shredded mozzarella
4 c. beef broth	cheese

Melt butter in a large skillet over medium heat. Add onion; cook for 15 to 20 minutes, until soft. Stir in sugar and salt; continue to cook and stir until golden. Add flour; mix well. Combine onion mixture, broth and wine or broth in a slow cooker. Cover and cook on high setting for 3 to 4 hours. Ladle soup into oven-proof bowls. Top with bread slices; sprinkle with cheeses. Broil until cheese is bubbly and melted. Serves 6.

There is not one blade of grass, there is no color in this world that is not intended to make us rejoice.

-John Calvin

Slowly-Simmered *Suppers*

Grama's Minestrone Soup

Lori Czarnecki
Milwaukee, WI

This is a recipe my grama used to make on the stovetop; however, I adapted it to the slow cooker. Double the recipe for a larger group, or just have delicious soup to enjoy for lunch the next day!

1/4 c. zesty Italian salad
   dressing
1 c. onion, chopped
1/2 c. celery, chopped
1/2 c. carrot, peeled and
   chopped
14-1/2 oz. can diced tomatoes

15-1/2 oz. can kidney beans,
   drained and rinsed
2 14-oz. cans vegetable broth
3 c. water
1 t. Italian seasoning
1-1/2 c. small shell macaroni,
   uncooked

Combine all ingredients except macaroni in a slow cooker; mix well. Cover and cook on low setting for 8 hours. Stir in macaroni; cover and cook on high setting for an additional 30 minutes, or until macaroni is tender. Serves 6.

MiMi's Corn Chowder

Rachel Hill
Center, TX

My daughter "adopted" a very special lady in our church, our pastor's wife. She started calling her MiMi, and since she makes the most wonderful corn chowder this is how it got its name!

3 slices bacon, crisply cooked
   and crumbled
1/4 c. onion, chopped
2 c. creamed corn
1 c. chicken broth
1 pt. light cream

6 saltine crackers, crushed
1 c. shredded Cheddar cheese
16-oz. pkg. frozen diced
   potatoes
salt and pepper to taste

Mix all ingredients together in a slow cooker. Cover and cook on low setting for 3 to 4 hours, until potatoes are tender. Serves 4 to 6.

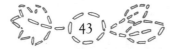

Slow-Cooker Honey Ribs

Darcy Ericksen
Independence, MO

Hearty and full of flavor.

10-1/2 oz. can beef broth
3/4 c. water
3 T. soy sauce
2 T. maple syrup
2 T. honey

2 T. barbecue sauce
1/2 t. dry mustard
2 lbs. baby back pork ribs,
    cut into serving-size pieces

Combine all ingredients except ribs in a slow cooker; mix well. Add ribs and stir to coat. Cover and cook on low setting for 6 to 8 hours, or on high setting for 3 to 4 hours. Serves 4.

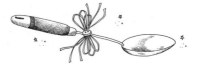

Pineapple Chicken

Debra Crosby
Elba, AL

Serve with rice and Chinese stir-fry vegetables for a great meal.

3 to 4 lbs. boneless, skinless
    chicken
16-oz. bottle Catalina salad
    dressing

20-oz. can pineapple chunks,
    drained and 1/4 cup juice
    reserved

Place chicken in slow cooker. Add salad dressing, pineapple and reserved juice. Cover and cook on high setting for 6 hours, or on low setting for 8 to 10 hours. Serves 4 to 6.

Make sure to use the right-size slow cooker...they cook their best when at least half of the crock is filled.

Slowly-Simmered *Suppers*

Slow-Cooker Goodness

Susan Shirron
Mars, PA

This is a thumbs-up recipe for our family. We love to use our slow cooker...especially on busy gymnastics nights.

4 boneless, skinless chicken
  breasts
4 boneless, skinless chicken
  thighs
2 1-oz. pkgs. ranch salad
  dressing mix

1/2 c. water
2 10-3/4 oz. cans cream of
  chicken soup
8-oz. pkg. cream cheese, cubed
12-oz. pkg. sliced mushrooms
16-oz. pkg. egg noodles, cooked

Place chicken into a lightly greased slow cooker. Combine salad dressing mix, water and soup; pour over chicken. Cover and cook on low setting for 3 to 4 hours. Stir in cream cheese and mushrooms; cover and continue to cook for an additional 45 minutes, or until chicken juices run clear. Shred chicken or serve whole over egg noodles. Spoon sauce from slow cooker over top. Makes 8 servings.

Invite friends over for a plant swap this fall...everyone goes home with a new plant and a start on their own friendship garden. Keep the menu easy...ask friends to tote along their favorite slow-cooker meal with the recipe for sharing.

Tomasso's Italian Beef

Jill Burton
Gooseberry Patch

My brother-in-law is from Italy and a fabulous cook!
He served this at a family reunion, where it was an instant hit.

10-3/4 oz. can tomato soup
10-1/2 oz. can beef broth
1/2 c. dry red wine or water
2 lbs. stew beef, cubed
14-1/2 oz. can diced Italian-
style tomatoes

3 carrots, peeled and cut into
1-inch pieces
1 t. Italian seasoning
1/2 t. garlic powder
2 16-oz. cans cannellini beans,
drained and rinsed

Combine all ingredients except beans in a slow cooker. Cover and cook on low setting for 6 to 8 hours, or on high setting for 3 to 5 hours. Stir in beans. Turn setting to high; cover and cook for an additional 10 minutes, or until beans are warmed through. Serves 8.

When filling kids' lunchboxes, chop a few extra carrots and celery. Keep frozen until they're needed for the next slow-cooker meal...ready when you are!

Slowly-Simmered *Suppers*

Apple-Raisin Ham

Patricia Wissler
Harrisburg, PA

This is just so yummy...a great way to use leftovers!

21-oz. can apple pie filling
1/3 c. golden raisins
1/3 c. orange juice
1/4 t. cinnamon

2 T. water
1-1/2 lbs. cooked ham,
    cut into 6 slices

Combine all ingredients except ham in a large bowl. Layer ham slices alternately with apple mixture in a slow cooker. Cover and cook on low setting for 4 to 5 hours. Makes 6 servings.

Cranberry Chicken

Dianne Taylor
Hayes, VA

Chicken with a sweet-tart flavor...really good!

3 to 4 lbs. chicken pieces
16-oz. can whole-berry
    cranberry sauce
1 c. barbecue sauce

1/2 c. celery, diced
1/2 c. onion, diced
1/2 t. salt
1/4 t. pepper

Combine all ingredients in a slow cooker. Cover and cook on low setting for 6 to 8 hours, or on high setting for 4 hours. Serves 6 to 8.

A quick harvest side dish...stir sautéed onions and garlic and chopped, toasted walnuts into hot, cooked rice.

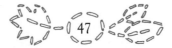

Molly's Tex-Mex Dinner

Angela Murphy
Tempe, AZ

My roommate tossed this together before leaving for an early-morning class. By lunchtime, it was ready, and tasted great!

3/4 c. cornmeal
1-1/2 c. milk
1 egg, beaten
1 lb. ground beef, browned
   and drained
1-1/4 oz. pkg. chili
   seasoning mix

1 t. seasoned salt
14-1/2 oz. can diced tomatoes
15-1/4 oz. can corn, drained
2-1/4 oz. can sliced black
   olives, drained
8-oz. pkg. shredded
   Mexican-blend cheese

Mix together cornmeal, milk and egg in a large bowl. Stir in remaining ingredients except cheese; spoon into a slow cooker. Cover and cook on high setting for 3 to 4 hours. Sprinkle with cheese; cover and continue to cook for an additional 5 to 10 minutes, until cheese melts. Serves 6.

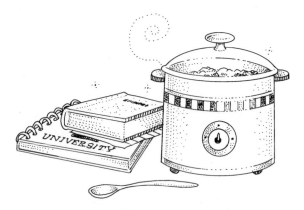

A slow cooker and super-simple recipes make the best college take-alongs. While students study or head out to class, they can come home knowing a hearty, home-cooked meal will be waiting when they return. That makes Mom feel good too!

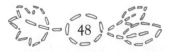

Slowly-Simmered *Suppers*

New England Chili

Shannon O'Donnell
East Wilton, ME

Great served over rice, in bread bowls or with cornbread.
Garnish with grated Cheddar cheese and sour cream.

2 lbs. ground turkey, browned
   and drained
1 onion, chopped
28-oz. can diced tomatoes
2 8-oz. cans tomato purée
2 16-oz. cans kidney beans

4-oz. can diced green chiles
1 t. garlic, minced
2 to 3 T. chili powder
2 t. salt
1 t. pepper

Spray a slow cooker with cooking spray. Combine all ingredients
in slow cooker. Cover and cook on low setting for 4 to 6 hours.
Serves 6 to 8.

Easy Chili Rellenos

Betty Kozlowski
Newnan, GA

My husband fell in love with this the first time he tasted it!

2 t. butter, softened
7-oz. can whole green chiles,
   drained and cut in strips
8-oz. pkg. shredded Cheddar
   cheese
8-oz. pkg. shredded Monterey
   Jack cheese

14-1/2 oz. can stewed tomatoes
4 eggs, beaten
2 T. all-purpose flour
3/4 c. evaporated milk

Spread butter in slow cooker. Layer chiles and cheeses; add tomatoes.
Stir together eggs, flour and milk; pour into slow cooker. Cover and
cook on high setting for 2 to 3 hours. Serves 6.

French Onion Pork Chops

Rebecca Ruff
Carthage, NY

Moist and tender...you'll love these pork chops!

4 pork chops
10-1/2 oz. can French
  onion soup

1/4 c. water
1 t. dried parsley
cooked egg noodles

Place pork chops in a slow cooker. Mix together soup and water; pour over chops. Sprinkle with parsley. Cover and cook on low setting for 6 to 8 hours. Serve over noodles. Makes 4 servings.

Mission Tour Pot Roast

Jackie Cannon
Princeton, KY

So good...this brings to mind Sunday dinners at Grandma's.

2 T. oil
3-lb. beef chuck roast
10-3/4 oz. can cream of
  mushroom soup
1-1/2 oz. pkg. onion soup mix

3 to 4 potatoes, peeled and
  quartered
2 to 3 carrots, peeled and
  quartered
Optional: cooked rice

Heat oil in a large skillet over medium heat; brown roast on both sides. Place roast in a slow cooker. Top with mushroom soup; sprinkle with onion soup mix. Cover and cook on low setting for 3 hours; add potatoes and carrots. Cover and continue cooking for an additional 5 to 6 hours. Serve over rice, if desired. Serves 4 to 6.

Let potluck guests know just what's cookin'...jot the recipe name on a mailing tag, then tie the tag to the knob on the slow cooker lid.

Slowly-Simmered *Suppers*

California Chicken Casserole

Conni Butler
Castaic, CA

This meal is a winner you can count on.

1/2 c. butter, diced
16-oz. pkg. frozen mixed
  vegetables, thawed
2 10-3/4 oz. cans cream of
  chicken soup
2 10-3/4 oz. cans cream of
  mushroom soup

1 T. garlic powder
1 T. onion powder
3 3-oz. pkgs. chicken-flavored
  ramen noodles
6 boneless, skinless chicken
  breasts, cut into bite-size
  pieces

Place butter in a slow cooker. Add vegetables and soups; mix well.
Sprinkle with garlic powder, onion powder and seasoning packets from
ramen noodles. Arrange chicken on top. Cover and cook on low setting
for 6 hours. Break ramen noodles into quarters; add to slow cooker.
(Reserve seasoning packets for another recipe.) Stir to cover noodles.
Cover and cook on high setting for one hour, until noodles are tender.
Serves 4 to 6.

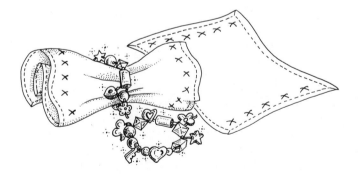

Roll napkins and slip a sparkly, elastic bracelet
around each for a napkin ring...fun!

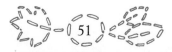

On-the-Road Soup

Megan Brooks
Antioch, TN

This is a regular on the menu when our family heads out in our RV.
The ingredients are tossed into the slow cooker first thing in the
morning, then we settle in to enjoy the scenery while dinner cooks.

2 c. water
15-1/4 oz. can corn, drained
1 c. potatoes, peeled and diced
1/2 c. carrots, peeled and diced
1/2 c. celery, diced
1/2 c. onion, diced
2 t. instant beef bouillon
   granules

16-oz. jar pasteurized process
   cheese sauce
2-1/2 t. hot pepper sauce,
   divided
1 lb. ground beef
1 egg, beaten
1/4 c. bread crumbs
1/2 t. salt

Combine first 8 ingredients in a slow cooker; stir in 2 teaspoons hot
pepper sauce. Combine ground beef, egg, bread crumbs, salt and
remaining hot pepper sauce; shape into meatballs. Add to slow cooker;
cover and cook on low setting for 6 to 8 hours. Serves 4 to 6.

Dress up the dinner table with some vintage whimsies!
While on vacation, check out local flea markets for
salt & pepper shakers in unusual shapes...dancing fruit,
hula girls and animals of all shapes and sizes will
really spark dinnertime conversations!

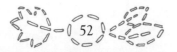

Slowly-Simmered *Suppers*

Southern BBQ Bean Soup

Tori Willis
Champaign, IL

When my daughter visited Alabama, this was one recipe she brought home...it's become a family favorite up north too!

16-oz. pkg. Great Northern
   beans, soaked overnight,
   drained and rinsed
3/4 c. onion, chopped
1/8 t. pepper

2 lbs. beef short ribs, cut into
   serving-size pieces
6 c. water
1 c. barbecue sauce
1 to 2 t. salt

Combine beans, onion, pepper and short ribs in a slow cooker; add enough water to cover. Cover and cook on low setting for 10 to 12 hours. Remove short ribs; cut meat from bones. Return meat to slow cooker; stir in barbecue sauce and salt to taste. Cover and cook on high setting for an additional 20 minutes, until warmed through. Serves 6 to 8.

Keep a kitchen garden right outside the door...filled with a variety of herbs, onions, peppers and garlic, they will be so handy (and fresh!) when preparing slow-cooker meals.

Slow-Cooker Pepper Steak

Debi Finnen
Berlin Heights, OH

This is a good recipe to make when onions and peppers
are plentiful in your backyard garden.

2 lbs. beef sirloin, cut into
   bite-size strips
garlic powder to taste
3 T. oil
1 cube beef bouillon
1/4 c. hot water
1 T. cornstarch

1/2 c. onion, chopped
2 green peppers, thinly sliced
14-oz. can stewed tomatoes
3 T. soy sauce
1 t. sugar
1 t. salt
cooked rice

Sprinkle beef with garlic powder. In a large skillet over medium heat, brown beef in oil. Transfer to a slow cooker. Mix together bouillon cube and water until dissolved; stir in cornstarch until dissolved. Pour over beef. Stir in remaining ingredients except rice. Cover and cook on low setting for 6 to 8 hours, or on high setting for 3 to 4 hours. Serve over rice. Serves 6.

No need to heat up the kitchen on an Indian summer day...
did you know your slow cooker can even bake potatoes?
In the morning, simply pierce potatoes with a fork and
wrap in aluminum foil. Cover and cook on low setting
for 8 to 10 hours...ready by dinnertime!

Slowly-Simmered *Suppers*

Diner-Style Burgers

Claire Bertram
Lexington, KY

There used to be a little diner in our town called Eloise's...it had the best food, always served with a smile. This is one of Eloise's specialties... people would come across town just to enjoy her cooking.

2 lbs. ground beef
1 egg, beaten
1 c. onion, finely chopped
1/2 c. shredded Cheddar cheese
2 T. catsup
2 T. evaporated milk
1/2 c. cracker crumbs
salt and pepper to taste
1 c. all-purpose flour
2 to 3 T. oil
10-3/4 oz. can cream of
   mushroom soup

Mix together ground beef, egg, onion, cheese, catsup, milk, cracker crumbs, salt and pepper. Shape into 8 patties; roll in flour. Heat oil in a large skillet over medium heat; brown patties. Arrange patties in a slow cooker alternately with soup. Cover and cook on high setting for 3 to 4 hours. Makes 8 servings.

Slow-cooker gravy...it's oh-so easy! When the meat is removed from the cooker, leave any juices inside. Make a smooth paste of 1/4 cup flour or cornstarch and 1/4 cup water. Pour into the slow cooker and stir well. Turn the cooker to the high setting and cook for 15 minutes once the mixture comes to a boil.

Rosemary-Garlic Tenderloins

Nola Coons
Gooseberry Patch

If the aroma isn't enough to pull you in, one bite and you'll find these turkey tenderloins amazingly moist and full of flavor.

1-1/4 c. white wine or
   chicken broth
1 onion, chopped
2 cloves garlic, minced
2 bay leaves
2 t. dried rosemary

1/2 t. pepper
3 turkey breast tenderloins
3 T. cornstarch
1/2 c. half-and-half or milk
1/2 t. salt

Combine wine or broth, onion, garlic and bay leaves in a slow cooker. Mix together rosemary and pepper; rub over turkey. Place in slow cooker. Cover and cook on low setting for 7 to 8 hours, or until a meat thermometer inserted in thickest part of turkey reads 170 degrees. Remove turkey and keep warm. Strain cooking juices into a saucepan. Combine cornstarch, half-and-half or milk and salt until smooth; gradually add to saucepan. Bring to a boil over medium heat; cook and stir for 2 minutes, until thickened. Remove and discard bay leaves. Slice turkey; serve with sauce. Serves 8.

When cooking a frozen roast or chicken, remember to add one cup of warm liquid to the cooker first. The liquid will act as a "cushion" to prevent sudden changes in temperature which might cause the cooker to crack. Be sure to add 4 to 6 hours cooking time on the low setting or 2 hours on high when frozen meats have been added to a recipe.

Slowly-Simmered *Suppers*

Spicy Mideastern Turkey

Katie Foster
Indianola, NE

So good...they'll be coming back for seconds!

1-1/2 lbs. boneless, skinless
 turkey tenderloins
1 green pepper, sliced
1-1/4 c. chicken broth, divided
1/4 c. soy sauce
2 cloves garlic, minced

3/4 t. red pepper flakes
2 T. cornstarch
1 onion, diced
1/3 c. creamy peanut butter
cooked vermicelli pasta

Combine turkey, green pepper, one cup broth, soy sauce, garlic and red pepper flakes in a slow cooker. Cover and cook on low setting for 3 to 4 hours, or until juices run clear. Mix cornstarch with remaining broth until smooth; stir into slow cooker. Add onion and peanut butter; mix well. Turn slow cooker to high setting; cover and cook for an additional 30 minutes. Serve over cooked vermicelli. Serves 4 to 6.

All the fun of autumn...a trip to the pumpkin patch, winding through a corn maze and a wagon ride in the countryside are all sure to stir up appetites. Come home to a hearty slow-cooked dinner that's ready when you are!

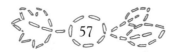

Garlicky Herbed Pork Roast

Nancy Wise
Little Rock, AR

*This recipe is one I know I can count on when I want
a dinner that's really special.*

4 to 5-lb. pork roast
4 cloves garlic, slivered
1 t. dried thyme
1/2 t. dried sage
1/2 t. ground cloves

1 t. salt
1 t. lemon zest
Optional: 2 T. cold water,
    2 T. cornstarch

Cut 16 small pockets into roast with a knife tip; insert garlic slivers.
Combine thyme, sage, cloves, salt and zest; rub over roast. Place roast
in a slow cooker. Cover and cook on low setting for 7 to 9 hours, or
on high setting for 4 to 5 hours. Allow roast to stand 10 to 15 minutes
before slicing. Remove and discard garlic pieces. If thicker gravy is
desired, strain juices into a saucepan over medium heat; bring to a
boil. Mix together water and cornstarch until dissolved; gradually add
to saucepan. Cook until thickened, about 5 minutes. Serve gravy over
sliced pork. Serves 8 to 10.

Grab your camera and notebook! Autumn is a fabulous time
to take a bike ride...snap some photos, gather leaves for
pressing and enjoy a sky that's as blue as a robin's egg!

Slowly-Simmered *Suppers*

Rosemary & Red Pepper Chicken
Valarie Dennard
Palatka, FL

An elegant main dish that's so easy to prepare.

1 onion, thinly sliced
1 red pepper, thinly sliced
4 cloves garlic, minced
2 t. dried rosemary
1/2 t. dried oregano
1/2 lb. Italian turkey sausage,
    casings removed
8 boneless, skinless chicken
    breasts

1/4 t. pepper
1/4 c. dry vermouth or
    chicken broth
2 T. cold water
1-1/2 T. cornstarch
salt to taste
Optional: 1/4 c. fresh parsley,
    chopped
cooked fettuccine

Combine onion, red pepper, garlic and herbs in a slow cooker. Crumble sausage over top. Arrange chicken over sausage; sprinkle with pepper. Pour in vermouth or broth; cover and cook on low setting for 5 to 7 hours. Transfer chicken to a platter; cover to keep warm. In a small bowl, stir together water and cornstarch. Stir into cooking liquid in slow cooker. Increase heat to high setting; cover and cook until sauce is thickened, stirring 2 to 3 times, about 10 minutes. Season with salt. Spoon sauce over chicken; sprinkle with chopped parsley, if desired. Serve with fettucine. Makes 8 servings.

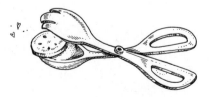

Crisp salads are super with slow-cooked dinners. Shake up the "usual" salad by mixing in some raisins, toffee-glazed almonds, crumbled feta or blue cheese, chow mein noodles or halved grapes...a tasty change of pace.

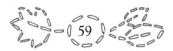

Beefy Vegetable Stew

Valerie Sovie
Ogdensburg, NY

This is a delicious hearty stew...my husband and I love to serve it with a warm crusty loaf of French bread. Prep time is short, which makes it a wonderful meal for days when we both have to work.

1-1/2 lbs. stew beef, cubed
3 potatoes, peeled and cubed
1 c. baby carrots
1 onion, coarsely chopped
1 clove garlic, minced
1 t. dried oregano
pepper to taste
12-oz. can regular or
   non-alcoholic beer

1-1/2 t. browning and
   seasoning sauce
2 T. beef soup base
3 T. butter, melted
3 T. all-purpose flour
1 c. frozen corn
1 c. frozen peas

Combine beef, vegetables, garlic, oregano and pepper in a slow cooker; pour beer over top. Add browning sauce and soup base; mix well. Cover and cook on low setting for 7 to 8 hours. About 30 minutes before serving, turn slow cooker to high setting. Blend together melted butter and flour; add to slow cooker. Stir in frozen peas and corn. Cover and cook on high setting for 20 to 30 minutes, stirring occasionally until vegetables are tender. Serves 4.

Keep a thermos of Beefy Vegetable Stew on hand for those chilly Friday night football games...sure to warm you up!

Slowly-Simmered *Suppers*

Debbie's Savory Roast Sandwiches

Debbie Fuls
Furnace, PA

This recipe is one I make for out-of-town guests.

3 to 4-lb. beef or pork roast	2 T. Worcestershire sauce
14-oz. bottle catsup	1 T. vinegar
1/2 c. taco sauce	1/8 t. dried oregano
1 onion, chopped	1/8 t. dry mustard
2 cloves garlic, pressed	1/8 t. pepper
2 T. brown sugar, packed	10 to 12 hard rolls, split

Place roast in a slow cooker; set aside. Mix together remaining ingredients except rolls; pour over roast. Cover and cook on low setting for 5 to 6 hours. Remove roast from slow cooker; shred with 2 forks. Return shredded meat to slow cooker; heat through and serve on rolls. Makes 10 to 12 sandwiches.

Slow-Cooked BBQ Chicken

Jennifer Fahs
Columbiana, OH

I like to serve this alongside steamed veggies.

4 to 6 boneless, skinless chicken breasts	1 lemon, thinly sliced
1 onion, thinly sliced	18-oz. bottle barbecue sauce
	3/4 c. cola

Combine all ingredients in a slow cooker; cover and cook on low setting for 8 hours. Shred chicken; stir back into sauce. Serves 4 to 6.

October is a symphony of permanence and change.

– Bonaro W. Overstreet

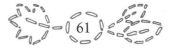

County Fair Italian Sausages

Dale Duncan
Waterloo, IA

Our family always heads to the Italian sausage food tent at the county fair...with this recipe, we can have them anytime!

19.76-oz. pkg. Italian pork
   sausages
1 green pepper, sliced
1 onion, sliced

26-oz. jar pasta sauce
5 sub buns, split
Garnish: 5 slices provolone
   cheese

Brown sausages in a non-stick skillet over medium heat; place in a slow cooker. Add pepper and onion; top with pasta sauce. Cover and cook on low setting for 4 to 6 hours. Place sausages in buns; top with sauce mixture and cheese. Makes 5 sandwiches.

Toast buns slightly before adding shredded or sliced meat,
or sausages or sandwiches...it only takes a minute
and makes such a tasty difference.

Slowly-Simmered *Suppers*

2-in-One Hoagies

Amanda Chitwood
Bedford, IN

One recipe, two delicious meals! Enjoy yummy hoagies tonight, then, by simply adding tomato juice, seasoned wild rice, green beans, corn and potatoes to taste, it's a scrumptious beef vegetable soup the next day!

3 lbs. stew beef, cubed
1.1-oz. pkg. beefy onion soup
  mix
3 to 4 green peppers, sliced 1/2-
  inch thick
12-oz. jar pepperoncini peppers,
  drained

1 T. beef soup base
1 t. garlic juice
5 c. water
10 to 12 hoagie rolls, split
10 to 12 slices Swiss cheese

Combine all ingredients except hoagie rolls and cheese in a slow cooker. Add water to about 2 inches from top. Cover and cook on low setting for 8 to 10 hours, or on high setting for 4 to 5 hours. Serve on rolls; top with cheese. Serve with cooking juices for dipping sauce. Makes 10 to 12 sandwiches.

Wrap 2-in-One Hoagies in aluminum foil and tuck in a basket with mini bags of potato chips, a couple of frosty sodas and a giant dill pickle from the deli...all you need for a tasty autumn picnic!

BBQ Country Ribs

Cynthia Dodge
Layton, UT

This recipe came together out of desperation as I was using up what items were in the freezer. These ribs taste great served with coleslaw and cornbread or rolls.

2 to 3 onions, quartered
3 to 4 lbs. country-style pork
  ribs, cut into serving-size
  pieces

1-1/2 c. barbecue sauce
28-oz. can baked beans

Arrange onions in a slow cooker; place ribs on top. Pour barbecue sauce over ribs. Cover and cook on low setting for about 8 hours, or until ribs are fork-tender. Stir in baked beans during last 20 to 30 minutes of cooking. Makes 4 to 6 servings.

Potato Lady Potatoes

Dixie Barkley
Hope Hull, AL

When I brought these potatoes to a church supper, they were a big hit. A few days later, a lady came up to me in the grocery store. She was so excited and said, "Aren't you the potato lady?" I had to write the recipe down for her right there!

4 15-oz. cans sliced potatoes,
    drained
2 10-3/4 oz. cans cream of
    celery soup

16-oz. container sour cream
1/2 lb. bacon, crisply cooked
  and crumbled
1 bunch green onions, sliced

Place potatoes in a slow cooker. Combine all remaining ingredients; add to potatoes and mix well. Cover and cook on low setting for 2 to 3 hours, stirring occasionally. Makes 12 to 15 servings.

Fireside **Favorites**

Around the Campfire

You can make the sweetest memories with family & friends when sitting around the campfire...it's easy!

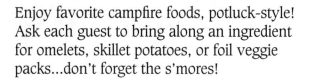

Enjoy favorite campfire foods, potluck-style! Ask each guest to bring along an ingredient for omelets, skillet potatoes, or foil veggie packs...don't forget the s'mores!

Bring some extra cozy quilts and throws for snuggling around the fire.

Kids enjoy putting on skits...let them plan the entertainment.

Mulled cider warms the soul. Take along a spice bundle of 3 cinnamon sticks, 2 tablespoons of whole cloves and a teaspoon of nutmeg wrapped together in cheesecloth. Warm 1/2 gallon of cider over the campfire with the spices for about 10 minutes...mmm!

Fireside Favorites

Up & At 'Em Omelet

Diana Chaney
Olathe, KS

*When we went camping in Colorado last summer, Mom packed all
the ingredients for these omelets. The recipe is so easy to whip up,
and since we each have our own pie iron, so simple to make.*

2 eggs, beaten
2 T. water
1/8 t. dried chives
salt and pepper to taste

2 to 3 T. vegetables, finely
  chopped
1 T. shredded Cheddar cheese

Beat together eggs and water. Add chives, salt and pepper. Pour into a
greased pie iron; top with vegetables. Close pie iron, latch handles and
grill over medium heat for about 2 minutes per side. Makes one serving.

Sunrise Skillet

Melody Taynor
Everett, WA

*When our kids wanted to camp out in the backyard, I just had to wake
them to the aroma of a delicious breakfast...this recipe does the trick
every time. They may be sleepy eyed, but they come running!*

1/2 lb. bacon
4 c. potatoes, peeled and cubed
1/2 onion, chopped

6 eggs, beaten
1 c. shredded Cheddar cheese
Optional: chopped green onions

Cook bacon in a cast-iron skillet over the slow-burning coals of a
campfire until crisply cooked. Remove bacon from skillet; set aside.
Stir potatoes and onion into drippings. Cover and cook until potatoes
are tender, about 10 to 12 minutes. Crumble bacon into potatoes. Stir
in eggs; cover and cook until set, about 2 minutes. Sprinkle with
cheese and green onions, if desired; let stand until cheese melts.
Serves 6 to 8.

Apple & Spice Baked French Toast

Andrea Beck
Boise, ID

French toast with a twist...yum! Put it together the night before, then bake and serve in the morning.

1 loaf French bread, sliced
8 eggs
3-1/2 c. milk
1 c. sugar, divided
1 T. vanilla extract
6 to 8 apples, peeled, cored
   and sliced
1 T. cinnamon
1 t. nutmeg
2 T. butter, diced
Garnish: warm maple syrup

Place bread in a greased 13"x9" baking pan; set aside. Beat eggs, milk, 1/2 cup sugar and vanilla together; pour half of mixture over bread. Layer apples over bread; pour remaining egg mixture over the top. Set aside. Combine remaining sugar, cinnamon and nutmeg; sprinkle over apples. Dot with butter; cover and refrigerate overnight. Bake, uncovered, at 350 degrees for one hour, until lightly golden. Remove from oven; let stand for 5 to 10 minutes before serving. Slice into squares and serve with warm maple syrup. Serves 8 to 10.

Campfire roasted apples are yummy! Core a cooking apple leaving the bottom of the apple intact. Fill the middle with one tablespoon each of butter and brown sugar and one teaspoon of cinnamon. Wrap in heavy foil and roast over the coals for 5 minutes per side. Let cool slightly, then enjoy.

Fireside Favorites

Cabin Supper

Amanda Lusignolo
Gooseberry Patch

_Last winter our family rented a little cabin out in the country...it was
so peaceful and quiet. After we came in from a friendly snowball fight,
all rosy-cheeked and frosty, I made this dish to warm us up...it worked!_

2 T. oil
1 onion, chopped
2 cloves garlic, minced
4 potatoes, peeled and cubed

1 lb. Kielbasa, cubed
4-oz. can chopped green chiles
15-oz. can corn, drained

Heat oil in a Dutch oven over medium heat; sauté onion and garlic
until tender. Add potatoes; cook for 20 minutes, stirring occasionally.
Add Kielbasa; cook and stir until potatoes are tender and golden,
about 10 minutes. Stir in chiles and corn; heat through. Serves 4 to 6.

Justin's Skillet Breakfast

Karen McCann
Marion, OH

_My son-in-law is an excellent cook. This was the first breakfast
he ever made for us...it's become a favorite in our family!_

1/2 lb. ground pork sausage
2 c. frozen shredded
    hashbrowns
10-oz. can diced tomatoes with
    green chiles, drained

8-oz. pkg. pasteurized process
    cheese spread, diced
6 eggs, beaten
2 T. water

Brown sausage in a large nonstick skillet over medium heat; drain.
Add hashbrowns and tomatoes. Cook for 5 minutes; sprinkle with
cheese. Beat eggs with water; pour evenly into skillet. Reduce heat to
low; cover and cook for 10 to 12 minutes, until eggs are set in center
and cheese is melted. Uncover; let stand 5 minutes before cutting into
wedges. Makes 6 servings.

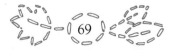

Jensen Family Hash

Kathy Jensen
Indianapolis, IN

I remember my mother and grandmother making this dish often. Now, my four grown daughters ask for the recipe for their own families.

2 T. margarine
16-oz. pkg. hot dogs, cut into
   bite-size pieces
1 onion, chopped

salt and pepper to taste
1/4 to 1/2 c. water
6 potatoes, cubed
2 to 3 T. catsup

Melt margarine in a large skillet over medium heat. Add hot dogs and onion; cook until onion is translucent. Sprinkle with salt and pepper. Stir in potatoes; add water. Cover and cook for 10 minutes, until potatoes are tender. Add catsup; stir to form a sauce and heat through. Serves 4 to 6.

Hot Dog Gravy & Biscuits

Jennifer Bean Bower
Winston-Salem, NC

One of my most favorite Saturday breakfasts. Whenever I had a slumber party, my mom would make this breakfast...my friends thought it was terribly delicious!

2-1/2 T. oil
16-oz. pkg. hot dogs, sliced
   1/4-inch thick
3 T. all-purpose flour

1/8 t. pepper
1-1 /2 c. milk
4 biscuits, split

Heat oil over medium heat in a large skillet. Add hot dogs and brown lightly. Stir in flour and pepper; mix well. Stir in milk; bring to a boil. Cook and stir until thickened; remove from heat. Serve over biscuits. Serves 4.

Fireside Favorites

Mexican Breakfast Bake

Eva Morgan
Chino Valley, AZ

We make this for breakfast whenever we're camping.

3/4 lb. ground pork sausage
1 doz. eggs, beaten
4-oz. can green chiles, drained
4-oz. can sliced mushrooms,
    drained

1 onion, chopped
1 loaf French bread
8-oz. pkg. shredded Mexican-
    blend cheese

Brown sausage in a large skillet over medium heat; drain. Add eggs, chiles, mushrooms and onion. Lower heat and cook until eggs are set. Slice bread in half horizontally; hollow out both halves, reserving removed bread for another use. Sprinkle cheese in bottom half of bread. Spoon egg mixture into bread; top with remaining bread half. Wrap in aluminum foil; heat through on the campfire. Serves 6.

The fragrance of coconut soap and coconut oil will keep pesky insects away...terrific take-alongs when camping.

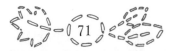

Campfire Jelly Biscuits

Lauren Geddings
Knoxville, TN

We spent many summer holidays tent camping in the Great Smoky Mountains. Part of our breakfast tradition always included my mother's famous campfire jelly biscuits. The biscuits are made from scratch and baked over the coals of the campfire. We would roll them out on floured wax paper covering the picnic table.

5 c. all-purpose flour
1 T. baking powder
1 t. baking soda
2 t. salt
1 c. shortening

1 env. active dry yeast
1/4 c. warm water
1-1/2 c. buttermilk
1/2 c. butter
1/2 c. strawberry preserves

While campfire coals are still glowing, lay a large rack across coals. Whisk together flour, baking powder, baking soda and salt. Cut in shortening. Dissolve yeast in warm water, about 110 to 115 degrees. Stir in buttermilk; add to dry ingredients. Stir well and knead, adding more flour if necessary. Roll out on floured wax paper to about one-inch thick. With a 3-inch round cookie cutter, cut out 10 biscuits. Spray a 9" round cake pan with cooking spray. Place biscuits in pan; cover tightly with aluminum foil. Place pan on rack over coals. Check for doneness after 20 minutes. Split biscuits; place a dollop of butter and preserves on each. Replace biscuit tops and wrap each biscuit in aluminum foil. Return to rack for 5 minutes, until butter melts and preserves are warm. Makes 10.

Don't tell fish stories where the people know you;
but particularly, don't tell them where they know the fish.

– Mark Twain

Fireside Favorites

Wyoming Praline Muffins

Trisha Donley
Pinedale, WY

These muffins are so yummy...great for a quick breakfast
or a Sunday brunch.

3 T. brown sugar, packed
1 T. butter, softened
1/3 c. chopped pecans
3 ripe bananas

1 egg, beaten
1/2 c. sugar
1/4 c. oil
1-1/2 c. pancake mix

Stir together brown sugar and butter in a small bowl; add pecans and set aside. In a separate bowl, mash bananas and stir in egg, sugar and oil until well blended. Add pancake mix; stir just until moistened. Fill greased muffin cups 2/3 full. Drop one teaspoon pecan mixture on top of each muffin. Bake at 350 degrees for 12 to 15 minutes, until golden. Makes one dozen.

Setting up just the right kind of campfire is easy...a tepee fire is terrific for quick cooking because the heat is concentrated in one spot, while a crisscross pattern is best for a long-lasting fire to enjoy all evening long.

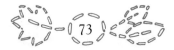

Wild West Quesadillas

April Jacobs
Loveland, CO

On a trip to the southwest, we stopped to camp at a little spot in the middle of nowhere. It was amazing...away from the city lights, the stars shone so bright. This pie-iron recipe was one we enjoyed more than once around the campfire.

1 lb. ground beef
1/2 c. onion, chopped
1-oz. pkg. taco seasoning mix
3/4 c. water
12 6-inch corn tortillas

1 c. shredded Monterey Jack
  cheese
Garnish: lettuce, diced tomato,
  salsa, sour cream

Brown ground beef and onion in a large skillet over medium-high heat; drain. Add taco seasoning and water; cook according to package directions. Spray the inside of a pie iron with non-stick vegetable spray; place a tortilla on one side. Spoon about 1/4 cup ground beef mixture on top of tortilla; sprinkle with cheese and top with onion. Place another tortilla on top; close pie iron. Cook over moderate heat until heated through and cheese is melted, about 3 to 6 minutes. Repeat with remaining ingredients to make 5 more. Garnish as desired. Makes 6 servings.

For quick & easy clean up, add a light coating of liquid soap to the outside of pots and pans before putting over the fire.

Fireside Favorites

Denise's Pizza Burgers

Denise Falls
New Berlin, WI

We love to camp, and this recipe is just another way to make burgers and camping fun!

2-1/2 lbs. ground beef
1/4 c. bread crumbs
1 T. dried basil
1 T. Italian seasoning
1/2 t. pepper
10 to 12 slices pepperoni, quartered

1/2 c. shredded mozzarella cheese
8-oz. jar pizza sauce, divided
8 to 10 slices mozzarella or provolone cheese
8 to 10 kaiser rolls, split

Mix together first 7 ingredients; add 1/4 cup pizza sauce. Shape into 8 to 10 patties. Grill on a hot grill to desired doneness. Warm remaining pizza sauce. Serve burgers on kaiser rolls, topping each with cheese and a spoonful of pizza sauce. Serves 8 to 10.

Dressed-Up Burgers

Ann Heavey
Bridgewater, MA

Make these burgers and your family & friends will rave!

2 lbs. ground beef
4-oz. container crumbled feta cheese
10 cherry tomatoes, halved

1 egg, beaten
1/2 c. fresh bread crumbs
1/2 t. salt
1 t. pepper

Mix together all ingredients; shape into 6 patties. Grill on a hot grill to desired doneness. Makes 6 servings.

Lakeside Fish & Veggies

Kelly Alderson
Erie, PA

The boys in our family just love to fish. We make this favorite supper with the catch of the day...it's easy to prepare and so delicious.

1 lb. fish fillets
2 cloves garlic, minced
1/2 t. dill weed
1/4 t. dry mustard
1 lemon, peeled, sliced
  and seeded

2 T. butter, diced and divided
3 potatoes, peeled and thinly
  sliced
16 baby carrots
1 stalk celery, diced
1/8 t. salt

Arrange fish fillets in the center of a length of lightly greased aluminum foil. Sprinkle with garlic, dill and mustard; arrange lemon slices over top. Arrange potatoes, carrots and celery around fish. Top vegetables with remaining butter; sprinkle with salt. Fold aluminum foil around fish and vegetables, sealing well. Grill 4 to 5 inches from medium-high heat for 25 to 35 minutes. Serves 4.

Homemade Tartar Sauce

Jackie Smulski
Lyons, IL

Top your favorite fish with this sauce...so easy and flavorful.

3 T. mayonnaise
2 T. bread-and-butter pickles,
  drained and minced

1 T. horseradish sauce
1/2 t. dill weed

Blend all ingredients together in a small bowl. Chill for 30 minutes. Makes about 1/3 cup.

Fireside Favorites

Campers' Beans

*Lisa Hays
Crocker, MO*

*For campers, it's dinner in a Dutch oven...simply prepare the recipe,
add to a Dutch oven and bury it in the coals for one to 2 hours.
We love these beans with cornbread and fried potatoes.*

6 to 8 slices bacon	2 T. mustard
1 onion, chopped	2 t. vinegar
1/4 c. brown sugar, packed	2 32-oz. cans baked beans
1/4 c. catsup	

Crisply cook bacon in a skillet over medium-high heat. When partially
cooked, add onion. Continue cooking until bacon is crisp. Drain bacon
and onion on a paper towel; crumble bacon. Combine brown sugar,
catsup, mustard and vinegar in a large saucepan; simmer over low
heat for 15 minutes. Stir in beans, bacon and onion. Simmer,
uncovered, for at least 30 minutes, stirring occasionally. If desired,
garnish with additional bacon. Makes 8 to 10 servings.

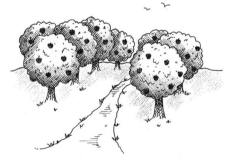

The smell of pine trees, the campfire glowing,
the marshmallows cooking, and the breath of crisp cool air
are some great things I like about camping. But my favorite
one of all is camping underneath the stars with light so
brilliant it brightens up the deep blue sky.

– Unknown

Mexican Cornbread

Melody Foutty
Geary, OK

This cornbread makes a great snack or serve it with chili. I send with my husband and sons when they go out camping...it doesn't last long.

1-1/2 lbs. ground pork sausage, browned and drained
3 8-1/2 oz. pkgs. cornbread mix
8-oz. pkg. shredded Cheddar cheese
14-3/4 oz. can creamed corn
2 jalapeño peppers, seeded and chopped
6 eggs, beaten
1 onion, chopped
3/4 c. milk

Mix together all ingredients in a large bowl. Pour into a lightly greased 13"x9" baking pan. Bake, uncovered, at 400 degrees for 40 to 45 minutes, until golden. Makes 12 to 15 servings.

Sausage & Black Bean Dinner

Sheila Gwaltney
Johnson City, TN

So easy and practically nothing to clean up...a winning recipe!

1 T. all-purpose flour
15-oz. can black beans, drained and rinsed
10-oz. pkg frozen corn, thawed
1 c. chunky salsa
1/2 lb. smoked pork sausage, sliced
1 c. shredded Colby-Jack cheese

Mix together all ingredients except cheese in a large bowl. Spoon onto 4 sheets of aluminum foil; fold into packets and seal well. Grill for 10 to 12 minutes, or bake on baking sheets at 400 degrees for 30 to 35 minutes. Sprinkle with cheese before serving. Serves 4 to 6.

Fireside Favorites

Canyon Grilled Veggies

Cathy Hillier
Salt Lake City, UT

Foil dinners are a sure bet when we go camping. And whether it's our annual trip to the Rocky Mountains, or camping out in our backyard, these foil-packet grilled veggies are always on the menu.

2 zucchini, halved lengthwise
   and thinly sliced
1 yellow squash, thinly sliced

3/4 c. butter, diced
garlic powder, salt and pepper
   to taste

Place zucchini and squash on a large sheet of aluminum foil. Dot with butter; sprinkle with seasonings to taste. Seal vegetables in foil. Place foil packet on a hot grill and cook for 20 minutes, until vegetables are tender. Makes 4 servings.

Dad's Potato Packets

Teresa Stiegelmeyer
Indianapolis, IN

My 83-year-young dad grills these potatoes alongside his burgers or steaks. No mess to clean up, just toss the aluminum foil!

1 T. olive oil
1 potato, peeled and cut
   into 1/2-inch strips
1/4 c. onion, sliced

1 T. butter, diced
salt and pepper to taste
1/4 c. shredded Colby cheese

Stack 2 aluminum foil sheets, one on top of the other. Pour oil in center. Layer remaining ingredients in order listed. Fold and seal aluminum foil to make a closed packet. Place on a medium-hot grill for about 30 minutes, until vegetables are tender. Serve in packet. Serves one.

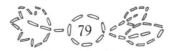

Fireside Reubens

Susie Backus
Delaware, OH

Reubens are one of my favorite sandwiches, so I tinkered around with a recipe I could grill whenever we're camping out. Now, I can enjoy my favorite sandwich anywhere!

8 slices pumpernickel bread
1 c. Thousand Island salad
   dressing

3/4 lb. deli sliced corned beef
1/2 lb. sliced Swiss cheese
1 c. sauerkraut, drained

Cut 4 large squares of aluminum foil. Place 2 slices of bread, side-by-side, on each piece of foil. Spread bread slices with salad dressing. Evenly divide corned beef, cheese and sauerkraut among bread. Top with a second slice of bread to make a sandwich. Wrap aluminum foil around sandwich; seal well. Place packets on a preheated grill over low heat. Cook, turning every 10 minutes, until bread is lightly toasted and cheese is melted, about 30 minutes. Makes 4 sandwiches.

Colorado Ham & Cheese

Barbara Duncan
Castle Rock, CO

These can also be assembled, then frozen...just heat as many as needed.

1/2 lb. cooked ham, shredded
1/2 lb. shredded sharp Cheddar
   cheese
2 eggs, hard-boiled, peeled and
   finely chopped
1/2 c. onion, finely chopped

1/2 c. green olives with
   pimentos, finely chopped
1/2 c. chili sauce
3 T. mayonnaise
16 hot dog buns, split

Combine first 5 ingredients; set aside. Mix together chili sauce and mayonnaise; add to ham mixture. Spoon into buns and wrap individually in aluminum foil. Bake at 375 degrees for 15 minutes, or until heated through. Makes 16 sandwiches.

Fireside Favorites

Mom's Potato Salad

Ann Christie
Glasgow, KY

This brings back memories of when my boys were young and we would take them camping at the lake. Their dad always built a big fire and this was one of the recipes I would prepare and take with us. My hint... if you mix everything together while the potatoes are warm, you'll get a nice, creamy consistency.

1 c. mayonnaise
1 t. mustard
1/2 t. celery seed
1/2 t. salt
1/8 t. pepper
4 c. potatoes, peeled, cooked
    and cubed

2 eggs, hard-boiled, peeled
    and chopped
1/2 c. onion, chopped
1/2 c. sweet pickles, drained
    and chopped

Combine mayonnaise, mustard, celery seed, salt and pepper in a large bowl; mix well. Add remaining ingredients; mix gently. Refrigerate until ready to serve. Serves 4 to 6.

Keep a block of ice in the cooler to chill food...it lasts so much longer than cubed ice.

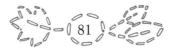

Girls' Camp Favorite

Emily Ansley
Lake City, FL

My sister brought this recipe home one summer from girls' camp when we were growing up. While they prepared it in aluminum foil packets over the campfire, it can also be a skillet supper.

1/4 c. beef broth or water, divided
2 to 3 potatoes, peeled and thinly sliced
garlic powder, salt and pepper to taste
2 carrots, peeled and thinly sliced
1 onion, chopped
1 lb. ground beef
1 T. butter, diced

Pour 2 tablespoons broth or water into a large skillet over medium heat. Spread potato slices in skillet; sprinkle with garlic powder, salt and pepper. Layer carrots and onion, then crumble ground beef over potatoes. Drizzle with remaining broth or water and sprinkle with additional seasonings, if desired. Dot with butter. Cover and cook over medium heat for 25 to 30 minutes, until potatoes are tender. Add additional broth or water during cooking, if necessary. Serves 2 to 4.

Camping or hosting a bonfire? Make it easy by preparing soups, stews or chili ahead of time. Just freeze and keep in a cooler, then reheat over the fire for a quick meal.

Fireside Favorites

Campers' Seasoning

Penny Sherman
Cumming, GA

Tote this along on your next camping trip...
it really adds flavor to steaks or burgers.

3 T. salt
3 T. paprika
2 T. pepper

1 T. garlic powder
1 T. onion powder
1 T. dried thyme

Combine all ingredients; mix well. Store in a small shaker jar. Makes about 3/4 cup.

Steak Onion Butter

Jennie Miller
Crystal Beach, FL

This is so yummy!

1/4 c. Bermuda onion, grated
1/4 c. fresh parsley, minced
1/4 c. butter, softened
1 t. Worcestershire sauce

1/2 t. salt
1/2 t. pepper
1/4 t. dry mustard

Blend all ingredients in a small bowl. Spread over steaks as you remove them from the grill or broiler. Makes about 3/4 cup.

When preparing foil packet dinners, add a few ice cubes to each packet to keep meat juicy.

Fruit Ripple Cookie Cake

Linda Smith
Daphne, AL

This is a great take-along for camping or picnics.

2 c. all-purpose flour
1-1/2 c. sugar
1/2 t. salt
4 eggs, beaten
1/2 c. butter, softened

1/4 c. oil
1-1/2 t. vanilla extract
1/2 t. cinnamon
21-oz. can favorite-flavor fruit
   pie filling

Combine all ingredients except pie filling in a large bowl; mix well. Spread half the batter in lightly greased 13"x9" baking pan. Top with pie filling; dollop remaining batter over top, covering as much of the filling as possible. Bake at 350 degrees for 40 to 45 minutes, until top is golden. Serve warm. Makes 12 to 15 servings.

Top off Fruit Ripple Cookie Cake...just punch the top of
a can of chocolate syrup, set in a skillet filled part-way
with water and warm over the coals. A swirl of sweetness
that's great for making fireside cocoa as well.

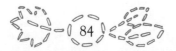

84

Fireside Favorites

Quick Trail Mix Bars

Susan Crouse
Sabillasville, MD

These treats are a hit with moms, and the kids love them too!

2 T. butter
1/2 c. creamy peanut butter
4 c. mini marshmallows

6 c. bran & raisin cereal,
   crushed
Optional: 1/4 c. chopped nuts

Combine butter and peanut butter in a microwave-safe bowl. Microwave on high setting for about one minute, or until melted. Stir and add marshmallows; toss to coat. Microwave for an additional one to 2 minutes. Stir and add cereal and nuts, if using; mix well. Press into a buttered 8"x8" baking pan. Cool for 30 minutes; slice into squares. Makes 16.

Maple Nut Bars

Francie Stutzman
Dalton, OH

These bars are so good because they have the added ingredient of chocolate chips...yummy!

1-1/2 c. all-purpose flour
2/3 c. sugar
3/4 c. butter
2 eggs, divided
14-oz. can sweetened
   condensed milk

1/4 t. maple flavoring
3/4 c. chopped nuts
3/4 c. semi-sweet chocolate
   chips

Mix flour and sugar together in a large bowl. Cut in butter until it has a crumbly appearance; stir in one egg. Pat into an ungreased 13"x9" baking pan. Bake at 350 degrees for 25 minutes. Combine condensed milk, remaining egg and maple flavoring; stir in nuts. Pour mixture over crust; sprinkle with chocolate chips. Bake for an additional 10 to 15 minutes, until golden and set. Cut into bars. Makes 16.

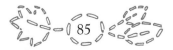

Gooey Marshmallow Cake

Staci Allen
Sheboygan, WI

This is a recipe my family enjoys in winter. We talk about all the wonderful memories we shared during our summer campouts and backyard fire pit adventures.

18-1/2 oz. pkg. yellow cake mix
2 eggs, beaten
1/2 c. oil
2 T. water

12-oz. pkg. semi-sweet chocolate chips
3-1/4 c. mini marshmallows

Mix together all ingredients in a large bowl. Pour into a lightly greased 13"x9" baking pan. Bake at 350 degrees for 20 minutes. Let cool; slice into squares. Serves 12 to 15.

Skillet S'mores

Mary Murray
Mt. Vernon, OH

Our kids love s'mores, so I tried to come up with a new way to make them. When I tossed the ingredients into a skillet, the kids laughed...but not after their first taste!

1 T. butter
10-oz. pkg. mini marshmallows
2 sleeves graham crackers,
   crushed

2 1-1/2 oz. chocolate candy bars, broken into pieces

Melt butter in a cast-iron skillet over slow, red campfire embers. Sprinkle in marshmallows; stir until completely melted. Remove from fire; stir in graham crackers and chocolate. Press into pan with the back of a spoon. Allow to cool completely; cut into wedges. Makes 10 servings.

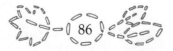

Fireside Favorites

Rachel's Chocolate Cheese Ball

Nicole Delaura
Cedar City, UT

This recipe was given to me by my best friend, Rachel. Her family in Utah makes this, and the recipe is famous...so famous, it's requested again & again by anyone who has ever tasted it!

2 8-oz. pkgs. cream cheese, softened
1-1/2 t. vanilla extract
12 chocolate sandwich cookies, crushed
1/2 c. powdered sugar
1 c. semi-sweet or milk chocolate chips
12-oz. pkg. chocolate or honey graham sticks

Combine first 4 ingredients in a medium bowl; mix well. Divide mixture in half; shape into 2 balls. Roll balls in chocolate chips; refrigerate until firm. Serve with graham sticks. Serves 8 to 10.

Sweet camping memories to treasure...bring a camera with plenty of film, flash and extra batteries. Why not let the kids each have their own disposable camera along with pen and paper? It'll be exciting to see what they liked best and can tuck into their own adventure photo journal!

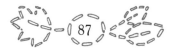

Dreamy Marshmallow Dip
Lisa Ann Panzino DiNunzio
Vineland, NJ

This fruit dip is wonderful for a family gathering, special event, summertime treat or camping snack.

8-oz. pkg. cream cheese
  softened
7-oz. jar marshmallow creme

2 T. strawberry, peach or
  pineapple jam
assorted fresh fruit

Blend cream cheese and marshmallow creme; gently stir in jam. Spoon into a pretty serving bowl; refrigerate for 2 to 4 hours. Serve with fruit for dipping. Makes about 2 cups.

Pack dips and sauces in little lidded Mason jars to take along to autumn picnics. Veggie and snack sticks are easy to dip right into the jars. Try pretzel sticks or apple slices with caramel dip and marshmallows with chocolate dip...yum!

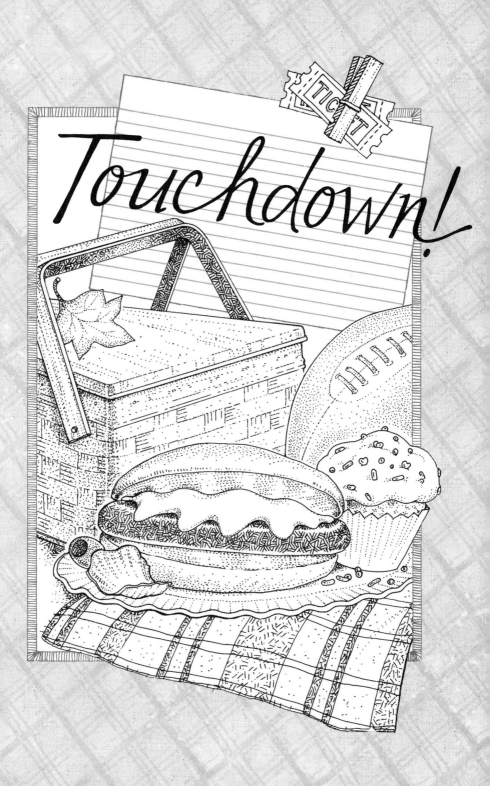

Touchdown!

Our top 5 tailgating must-haves...

A tent...you never know when
it will rain!

Two gallons of water...for quick & easy
clean up and to extinguish the grill.

Chairs and folding tables...for comfy
seating and a spot to arrange food, slow cookers,
flatware, plates and napkins.

Comfortable shoes...for visiting
with friends & neighbors.

A camera...to
capture all the game-day fun!

Touchdown!

Deluxe Cocktail Sausages

*Carrie Helke
Schofield, WI*

*These sausages are so simple to make. They're sure
to be a hit at your next tailgate party!*

1/2 c. butter
3 T. brown sugar, packed
3 T. honey
1/2 c. chopped pecans

8-oz. tube refrigerated crescent
   rolls, separated
24 mini smoked cocktail
   sausages

Preheat oven to 400 degrees. As oven is warming, melt butter in oven in a 13"x9" glass baking pan. When butter is melted, add brown sugar, honey and pecans; stir to coat bottom of the pan. Slice each crescent roll triangle into thirds. Roll each smaller triangle around one sausage. Place on butter mixture, seam-side down. Bake, uncovered, at 400 degrees for 15 minutes, or until golden. Makes 2 dozen.

Keep tailgating decorations whimsical...mascot blow-ups, foam fingers and colorful banners will help everyone know just how to find your party.

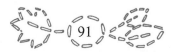

The Best-Yet Buffalo Wings

Kristen Taylor
Fort Smith, AR

These wings are sweet, but the sauce is hot!

3 lbs. chicken wings
seasoned salt to taste
2-oz. bottle hot pepper sauce

1 c. water
1 c. brown sugar, packed
1 T. mustard seed

Arrange chicken wings on a 15"x10" jelly-roll pan sprayed with non-stick vegetable spray. Bake at 400 degrees for 20 minutes; turn wings. Bake for an additional 20 to 30 minutes, until golden and juices run clear; drain. Sprinkle with seasoned salt; arrange on serving platter. Combine hot pepper sauce, water, brown sugar and mustard seed in a saucepan; bring to a boil over medium heat. Reduce heat to low; cook until mixture caramelizes and becomes a dark burgundy color, stirring occasionally. Pour sauce over wings before serving, or serve on the side for dipping. Makes about 3 dozen.

It's easy to enjoy warm cider at the tailgate! Warm up hot drinks just before you leave and bring along in an insulated jug.

Touchdown!

Sweet Mesquite Glazed Wings

Mike Robinson
Hominy, OK

Our family loves chicken and is always looking for new ways to prepare it. These wings are a big hit every year during football season...they rank in the top 5 of the most requested appetizers!

5 lbs. chicken wings
2 T. oil
1/4 c. mesquite seasoning,
   divided

1 c. maple syrup
2 T. lemon juice

Combine wings with oil in a large bowl; toss to coat evenly. Sprinkle with one tablespoon seasoning; toss to coat evenly. Combine syrup, lemon juice and remaining seasoning; set aside. Grill wings over medium-high heat for 15 to 18 minutes, or until juices run clear, turning often. Remove from grill; drizzle with half of syrup mixture. Serve remaining syrup mixture as a dipping sauce. Makes about 5 dozen.

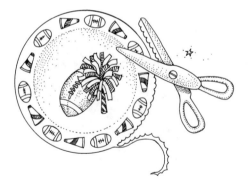

Decorative-edge scissors are a quick & easy way to dress up paper plates and napkins for a football Friday night...just rim around the edges.

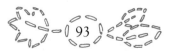

Championship Meatballs

David Wink
Gooseberry Patch

*With only 3 ingredients, these meatballs are a snap to prepare,
and the flavors blend to make the most amazing sauce.*

1 lb. ground pork sausage
1/2 c. apple butter

1-1/2 T. maple syrup

Form sausage into one-inch balls; place on a microwave-safe plate.
Cover and microwave on high setting for one to 2 minutes, or until a
meat thermometer reads 160 degrees; drain. Cool; place in a plastic
zipping bag. Combine apple butter and syrup; pour over meatballs.
Refrigerate overnight. Shortly before serving, transfer meatballs and
sauce to a microwave-safe serving dish. Cover and microwave on
high for one minute, or until heated through. Serve immediately.
Makes 8 servings.

Use clip-style clothespins to secure a few favorite
tailgating recipes together...ideal for sharing with
friends during the big game.

Touchdown!

Mom's City "Chicken"

Margaret Cabaj
Sebring, FL

This recipe is one my mom made, and now I've been making for
51 years...tasty served warm from the oven or even cold.

2 lbs. beef round steak, cubed
3 lbs. pork steak, cubed
salt and pepper to taste

1 to 2 c. all-purpose flour
shortening for frying
1/4 t. garlic powder

Thread beef and pork alternately onto metal skewers. Sprinkle with
salt and pepper; dredge in flour. Melt shortening in a large skillet
over medium heat; brown meat on all sides. Place meat in a greased
roaster pan with lid; sprinkle with garlic powder. Bake, covered,
at 325 degrees for 1-1/2 hours. Serves 8 to 10.

Pick the day...enjoy it to the hilt!

–Audrey Hepburn

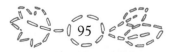

End-Zone Layered Taco Dip

Angela Moore
State College, PA

Cheer your team on to win the championship with these tacos...
an all-time favorite. Is it dip, is it salad? You choose!

1 lb. ground turkey
1-1/4 oz. pkg. taco
   seasoning mix
3/4 c. water
8-oz. pkg. cream cheese,
   softened
16-oz. container sour cream
16-oz. jar container salsa

1 head lettuce, chopped
1 c. shredded Cheddar cheese
1 green pepper, chopped
1 red pepper, chopped
2-1/4 oz. can sliced black
   olives, drained
corn chips

Brown ground turkey in a skillet over medium heat; drain. Add taco
seasoning and water; simmer 5 minutes. Remove from heat; cool. In a
bowl, mix together cream cheese and sour cream until smooth. Spread
cream cheese mixture directly onto an ungreased pizza pan; spread
salsa over top. Layer in the following order: lettuce, cheese, peppers,
olives and turkey mixture. Serve immediately or chill until serving.
Serve with corn chips. Makes 12 servings.

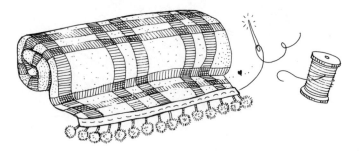

Fleece is so easy to cut and sew, even the littlest ones in
the family can create a blanket in school colors. Just
trim the fleece to size, then cut fringe or stitch
pompoms along the edges.

Touchdown!

Cheer-'Em-On Spread

Kathy Grashoff
Fort Wayne, IN

This southwestern-style spread is so good...the addition of corn along with walnuts really makes it flavorful!

2 8-oz. pkgs. cream cheese, softened
1/4 c. lime juice
4-oz. can chopped green chiles
3 green onions, thinly sliced
1 T. ground cumin
1 t. cayenne pepper
1/2 to 1 t. salt
1 t. pepper
8-3/4 oz. can corn, drained
Optional: 1 c. chopped walnuts
tortilla chips

Combine cream cheese and lime juice: mix until smooth. Beat in chiles, onions and seasonings; stir in corn and walnuts, if using. Cover and refrigerate for at least 4 hours. Serve with tortilla chips. Makes 3 cups.

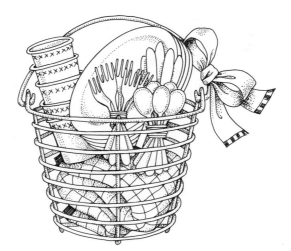

Tin pails or egg baskets are perfect for toting goodies to and from a tailgating party. They're roomy enough to hold paper plates, cups, napkins and a tablecloth.

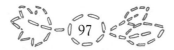

Laura's Chicken Pesto Pizza

Laura Witham
Anchorage, AK

I absolutely love to cook...The Food Network is on at my house all the time. When my husband and I ordered a chicken pizza with pesto at a restaurant, we both fell in love with the flavor. After months and months of experimenting with different ingredients, I was able to recreate my version of this wonderful pizza.

2 boneless, skinless chicken breasts
1 T. olive oil
13.8-oz. tube refrigerated pizza dough
7-oz. jar pesto sauce
3 T. tomato sauce

14-1/2 oz. can petite diced tomatoes, drained
salt to taste
8-oz. pkg. shredded mozzarella cheese
2 T. Italian seasoning

In a skillet over medium heat, brown chicken in oil. Remove to cutting board to cool; chop finely and set aside. Spread dough out onto a greased baking sheet; pierce surface of dough with a fork. Mix together pesto, sauce and tomatoes; add salt to taste. Stir in chicken; mix well. Spread over pizza dough; top with cheese and Italian seasoning. Bake for at 400 degrees for 10 to 12 minutes, until cheese is melted and bubbly. Makes 6 to 8 servings.

Invite friends to a tailgating potluck and be sure to ask them to bring along copies of their recipes...a super way to share game-day favorites!

Touchdown!

Garlic-Romano Dipping Sauce

Denise Mainville
Huber Heights, OH

This sauce is also delicious over vegetables, and if you add a bit of balsamic vinegar, you've got a very tasty salad dressing.

1 c. grated Romano cheese
1/4 t. red pepper flakes
1/2 c. olive oil

1 clove garlic, pressed
1 loaf Italian bread, cubed

Whisk together cheese, red pepper flakes, oil and garlic in a small bowl; mix until well combined. Refrigerate until ready to serve. Bring sauce to room temperature before serving with bread. Makes 1-1/2 cups.

Upcountry Party Spread

Ralice Gertz
Greensboro, NC

This recipe was given to me by a dear friend about 8 years ago.

6 slices bacon, crisply cooked
and crumbled
1 c. shredded sharp Cheddar
cheese
1 c. grated Parmesan cheese

1 c. mayonnaise
1/4 c. onion, finely chopped
1/8 t. garlic powder
2-oz. pkg. slivered almonds
assorted crackers

Combine all ingredients except crackers in a medium bowl; mix well. Serve with crackers. Makes 15 servings.

Quarterback Sneaks

Carol Lytle
Columbus, OH

*My daughter caught her 3-year-old brother sneaking these appetizers
out of the refrigerator the day of a big Ohio State bowl game
championship...that's how they got this silly name!*

8-oz. pkg. cream cheese,
  softened
2 T. mayonnaise
1 T. onion, grated
1 T. onion juice

1 loaf white bread, sliced and
  crusts trimmed
22-oz. jar whole baby dill
  pickles, drained

Blend together cream cheese, mayonnaise, onion and onion juice in a
medium bowl. Thinly spread on bread slices. Roll one pickle in each
slice of bread; arrange seam-side down in an ungreased 13"x9" baking
pan. Cover and chill for 8 hours, or overnight. To serve, slice each roll
into one-inch slices. Makes 14 servings.

Salad that's just right for a tailgate. Serve tossed salad in
a clean, insulated beverage cooler. Just pop the top open
and add tongs for easy serving, right out of the "box."

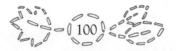

Touchdown!

Swiss & Rye Bites

Jo Ann
Gooseberry Patch

These have been on our tailgating menu as long as I can remember. They never last long, and are so easy to prepare, I've been known to make extra batches at halftime!

2.8-oz. can French fried
   onions, crushed
3/4 c. bacon, crisply cooked
   and crumbled

1/2 c. mayonnaise
3 c. shredded Swiss cheese
14-oz. jar pizza sauce
1 loaf sliced party rye

Combine onions, bacon, mayonnaise and cheese in a large bowl. Spread one teaspoon pizza sauce on each slice of bread; top with one tablespoon cheese mixture. Arrange on an ungreased baking sheet. Bake at 350 degrees for 12 to 14 minutes, until heated through and cheese is melted. Serves 6.

Don't forget finger foods for the kids...tortilla pinwheels and mini pigs-in-a-blanket are great for little tailgaters.

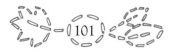

Francie's Cheddar Squares

Francie Stutzman
Dalton, OH

This recipe makes enough to satisfy even the biggest football crowd!

1/2 c. butter, softened
16-oz. pkg. shredded Cheddar
   cheese
3 c. milk

3 eggs, beaten
salt and pepper to taste
10 slices bread, crusts trimmed

Mix together butter and cheese in a double boiler. Heat milk to almost boiling in a large saucepan over medium heat; add to cheese mixture. Heat until cheese melts. Stir in eggs and seasonings. Arrange bread slices in 2 rows in an ungreased 13"x9" baking pan. Slowly pour cheese mixture over top. Refrigerate overnight. Bake at 350 degrees for 35 to 45 minutes. Cut into one-inch squares. Makes about 9 dozen.

Apple-Cheese Fondue

Weda Mosellie
Phillipsburg, NJ

Scrumptious for any occasion!

1 clove garlic, minced
1 c. dry white wine or
   apple juice
1/2 lb. Gruyère cheese,
   shredded
1/2 lb. Swiss cheese, diced
2 T. cornstarch

1/8 t. nutmeg
1/8 t. pepper
1 French baguette, torn into
   bite-size pieces
2 apples, cored, quartered
   and sliced

In a fondue pot or saucepan over medium heat, combine all ingredients except bread and apples. Bring to a simmer, stirring constantly, until cheese is melted. Serve with baguette and apple pieces for dipping. Makes 4 servings.

Touchdown!

Aloha Dip

Deena Seegars
Pace, FL

*You will always be asked again & again to bring this
yummy dip to tailgating get-togethers!*

1 loaf Hawaiian bread
8-oz. pkg. cream cheese,
   softened
16-oz. container sour cream
1 bunch green onions, chopped

8-oz. pkg. shredded Cheddar
   cheese
1/2 lb. deli honey ham, chopped
   into bite-size pieces
1/4 c. Worcestershire sauce

Slice top off bread. Scoop out inside of loaf; reserve bread pieces and set aside. Mix together cream cheese and sour cream; stir in remaining ingredients. Spoon into bread bowl. Replace top of bread; set on a baking sheet. Bake at 250 degrees for one hour. Remove lid; stir gently. Bake for an additional 30 minutes. Serve with reserved bread. Makes 12 to 15 servings.

Party supply stores have a variety of decorations to get tailgaters in the spirit of the game...be sure to pick up some pompoms, megaphones, sparklers and a CD of band music!

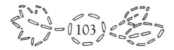

Savory BBQ Muffins

Elizabeth Cisneros
Chino Hills, CA

Great for a game-day brunch, or alongside munchies at half-time.

3/4 lb. ground beef, browned
   and drained
1/2 c. barbecue sauce
1 t. white vinegar
2 T. brown sugar, packed
1/8 t. salt

1/8 t. garlic powder
1 red pepper, finely chopped
1/2 red onion, finely chopped
1 c. shredded Cheddar cheese
8-oz. tube refrigerated biscuits

Combine beef, sauce, vinegar, brown sugar, salt and garlic powder. Stir in red pepper and onion. Press biscuits into bottom and up sides of lightly greased muffin cups. Spoon meat mixture into biscuit cups; sprinkle with cheese. Bake at 400 degrees for 10 to 15 minutes, until biscuits are golden. Makes 8.

Fly a bunch of helium-filled balloons on the truck bumper so friends can find you... no matter how crowded the stadium parking lot may be!

Touchdown!

6-Layer Halftime Dip

Renee Johnson
Smithville, TN

No matter what the get-together, this dip is a favorite of all ages!

1-1/2 c. cream cheese, softened
1-1/2 c. cooked chicken, chopped
1 c. green onions, chopped
3/4 c. ranch or blue cheese salad dressing

1/4 c. butter, melted
3/4 c. hot wing sauce
1-1/2 c. shredded sharp Cheddar cheese
tortilla chips, celery sticks

Spread cream cheese in a 13"x9" baking pan. Sprinkle with chicken; top with green onions. Spread dressing evenly over green onions. Combine butter and sauce; drizzle over top. Sprinkle with cheese; bake at 350 degrees for 15 to 20 minutes, until cheese melts. Serve with tortilla chips and celery sticks. Makes 12 servings.

Cheesy Jalapeño Dip

Amber Cave
Ballinger, TX

This dip is a must-have when my Bible study group meets.

8-oz. pkg. cream cheese, softened
1 c. shredded Cheddar cheese
1/4 c. mayonnaise
5-oz. can deviled ham
2 T. onion, minced

1 T. spicy brown mustard
1 to 2 T. jalapeño peppers, finely chopped
1 t. dried parsley
assorted crackers

Combine all ingredients except crackers in a large mixing bowl. Blend with an electric mixer on medium speed. Chill until ready to serve. Serve with crackers. Makes about 2 cups.

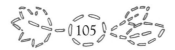

Ranch Ham & Tortilla Pinwheels

Lisa Johnson
Hallsville, TX

These are a favorite of all ages.

1 c. deli smoked ham, cubed
2 8-oz. pkgs. cream cheese,
  softened
.4-oz. pkg. ranch salad
  dressing mix
2 green onions, minced

4 12-inch flour tortillas
4-oz. can diced green chiles,
  drained
Optional: 2-1/4 oz. can sliced
  black olives, drained

Mix together ham, cream cheese, dressing mix and green onions;
spread on tortillas. Sprinkle with chiles and olives, if using. Roll
tortillas tightly. Chill at for least 2 hours, or overnight. Slice rolls into
one-inch pieces. Makes 3 dozen.

Bring the football field right to your tailgate! Line the
truck bed with green outdoor carpeting...easily found
at a do-it-yourself hardware store.

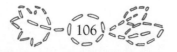

Touchdown!

Seafood Pinwheels

Wendy Lee Paffenroth
Pine Island, NY

I like to put a little slice of Muenster cheese over each pinwheel before I bake them, then place the pinwheels under the broiler for about 30 seconds until the cheese is golden.

8-oz. pkg. cream cheese,
  softened
6 to 8 ozs. imitation crabmeat,
  shredded
1/2 c. red pepper, chopped
1/2 c. shredded Cheddar cheese

2 green onions, chopped
1/4 c. fresh parsley, chopped
1/2 to 1 t. hot pepper sauce
chili powder to taste
6 6-inch flour tortillas
Garnish: paprika

Beat cream cheese until smooth; stir in crabmeat, red pepper, shredded cheese, onions, parsley and sauce. Sprinkle with chili powder; stir until well blended. Spread cheese mixture evenly over tortillas; roll up tightly. Slice off ends; wrap in plastic wrap. Refrigerate for 2 hours, or overnight. When ready to serve, slice each roll into 6 slices. Arrange on a baking sheet sprayed with non-stick vegetable spray. Bake at 350 degrees for 10 to 12 minutes, or until bubbly. Sprinkle with paprika; serve warm. Makes about 3 dozen.

Thanksgiving dinners take eighteen hours to prepare. They are consumed in twelve minutes. Halftimes take twelve minutes. This is not a coincidence.

– Erma Bombeck

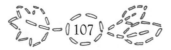

Buckeye Blitz Mix

Brenda Smith
Delaware, OH

When The Ohio State Buckeyes take to the field, our family is sure to have this savory popcorn mix on hand for munching.

1/4 c. butter, melted
1 t. paprika
1/2 t. red pepper flakes

1/2 t. ground cumin
10 c. popped popcorn
1/3 c. grated Parmesan cheese

Combine butter and spices; toss with popcorn. Sprinkle with Parmesan cheese; toss to mix. Makes about 10 cups.

Karen's Cayenne Pretzels

Karen Boehme
Greensburg, PA

These spicy-hot pretzels were the hit of the party when our Pittsburgh Steelers became champs!

1 c. oil
1-oz. pkg. ranch salad
   dressing mix

1 t. garlic salt
1-1/2 t. cayenne pepper
2 10-oz. pkgs. pretzel twists

Mix together first 4 ingredients; pour over pretzels in a large bowl. Stir until well coated; spread onto ungreased baking sheets. Bake at 200 degrees for 1-1/4 hours to 1-1/2 hours. Makes 8 to 10 cups.

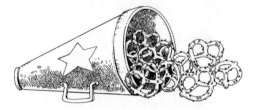

A megaphone or new football helmet makes a clever serving bowl for snack mixes!

Touchdown!

Cinnamon-Glazed Pecans
Beth McCallister
Barboursville, WV

These taste just like the yummy pecans you can enjoy at a fair or mall.

2 egg whites
2 T. water
2 T. vanilla extract
1 lb. pecan halves

1-1/2 c. powdered calorie-free
   sweetener
1 T. salt
3 T. cinnamon

Beat together egg whites, water and vanilla until foamy; pour over pecans in a large bowl. Add remaining ingredients; stir well. Spread in a single layer on a lightly greased baking sheet. Bake at 350 degrees for about 45 minutes, or until crunchy, stirring frequently. Cool. Makes about one pound.

Toasted Almonds with Rosemary
Denise Mainville
Huber Heights, OH

If you don't have fresh rosemary, you can substitute one teaspoon dried rosemary...just be sure to crush it first.

2 c. whole almonds
1 T. olive oil

1 T. fresh rosemary, chopped
1/4 to 1/2 t. salt

Spread nuts on a baking sheet; drizzle with oil and toss to coat. Sprinkle with rosemary and salt; stir to coat. Spread in a single layer. Bake at 350 degrees for 10 to 15 minutes, until nuts are toasted, stirring every 5 minutes. Remove from pan; spread on aluminum foil to cool. Makes 2 cups.

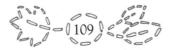

"Go Team!" Sub Salad

Kathleen Felton
Fairfax, IA

Make sure you have the recipe with you wherever you go.
You'll get lots of requests for this one!

1 head lettuce, shredded
2 kaiser rolls, torn into
  1/2-inch pieces
1/2 to 1 lb. assorted sliced deli
  meats such as ham, turkey,
  salami and bologna, sliced
  into strips
1/4 to 1/2 lb. Swiss cheese,
  sliced into strips

1/4 to 1/2 lb. Cheddar cheese,
  sliced into strips
3-oz. pkg. sliced pepperoni
1 red onion, chopped
1/2 c. olive oil
1/4 c. tarragon vinegar
1 t. garlic salt
1/4 t. pepper

In a large bowl, mix together lettuce, bread, meats, cheeses and onion. In a separate bowl, whisk together oil, vinegar, garlic salt and pepper. Mix well; drizzle over salad, tossing to coat. Refrigerate for one hour. Serves 8 to 10.

Deflated footballs make oh-so clever serving bowls...
just line with a napkin and fill with potato chips,
pretzels or tortilla chips.

Touchdown!

Pepperoni Pizza Muffins

Andrea Gordon
Lewis Center, OH

These serve-yourself muffins are great for a crowd.

1-1/3 c. all-purpose flour
1 c. whole-wheat flour
1 t. baking soda
1/2 t. Italian seasoning
1 t. pizza seasoning
1-3/4 c. spaghetti sauce
1/4 c. milk

3 T. olive oil
1 egg, beaten
1-1/2 c. pepperoni, chopped
8-oz. pkg. shredded mozzarella
  cheese
1/2 to 1 c. grated Parmesan
  cheese

Mix together all ingredients. Fill lightly greased muffin cups 2/3 full.
Bake at 400 degrees for 20 minutes. Makes one dozen.

Trilby

Margaret Bean
Glenpool, OK

This is a recipe that was given to me by my sister. I make it often for holidays and special get-togethers.

6 eggs, hard-boiled and peeled
2 to 3 green onions, chopped
1 t. paprika
8-oz. pkg. shredded sharp
   Cheddar cheese
1 t. garlic salt
1 t. dried parsley
1/4 to 1/2 c. mayonnaise
assorted crackers

Mash hard-boiled eggs. Add remaining ingredients except crackers; mix well. Add enough mayonnaise to be spreadable. Serve with crackers. Makes 10 to 12 servings.

Curried Chutney Spread

Lynda Robson
Boston, MA

I like to add a bit more curry just because I love the flavor.

8-oz. pkg. cream cheese,
   softened
2 T. sour cream
1 t. curry powder
1/2 c. green onions, sliced
1/2 c. chopped peanuts
9-oz. jar chutney

In a small bowl, beat together cream cheese, sour cream and curry powder until smooth. Fold in onions and peanuts. Spread about 1/2-inch thick on a serving plate. Chill until ready to serve. Just before serving, spread chutney over top. Serve with crackers. Makes 12 servings.

Touchdown!

Tailgate Sandwich Ring

Crystal Vogel
Springdale, PA

*I make this for all my tailgating parties...my husband
and friends request it all the time.*

2 11-oz. tubes refrigerated
  French bread dough
1/2 lb. bacon, crisply cooked
  and crumbled
3/4 c. mayonnaise
1 T. green onion, chopped

1/2 lb. deli sliced turkey
1/2 lb. deli sliced ham
1/2 lb. sliced provolone cheese
2 tomatoes, sliced
2 c. lettuce, chopped

Spray a Bundt® pan with non-stick vegetable spray. Place both tubes
of dough into pan, seam-side up, joining ends together to form one
large ring. Pinch edges to seal tightly. Lightly spray top of dough with
non-stick vegetable spray. Bake at 350 degrees for 40 to 45 minutes,
until golden. Carefully turn out; cool completely. Combine bacon,
mayonnaise and onion; mix well. Slice bread horizontally. Spread
half the bacon mixture over bottom half of bread. Top with turkey,
ham and provolone. Place on an ungreased baking sheet. Bake at
350 degrees until cheese melts. Top with tomatoes and lettuce. Spread
remaining bacon mixture on top half; place over lettuce. Slice into
wedges. Serves 8.

Consider creating your own tailgate
party invitations by cutting football
shapes out of corrugated cardboard.
Jot the party particulars on the back
and trim it with white shoe laces
woven through punched holes.

Donna's Juicy Burgers

Donna Jones
Mikado, MI

My family loves grilled burgers in the summer, and with some experimenting, we came up with a recipe for burgers that are always a hit. This recipe also makes a delicious meatloaf for days when grilling isn't possible.

2 lbs. ground beef
1 c. Italian-seasoned bread
   crumbs
1 onion, chopped
2 to 3 cloves garlic, minced

2 eggs, beaten
1/2 to 1 t. salt
1/8 t. pepper
8 sandwich buns, split

Mix together all ingredients well; form into patties. Grill burgers over medium heat to desired doneness. Makes about 8 burgers.

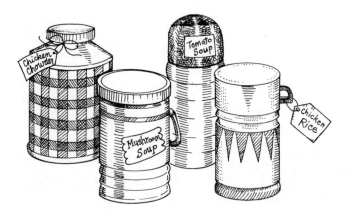

Keep a variety of thermoses on hand and fill each with
a different warming soup or stew...so easy to tote along
and share during a chilly fall game.

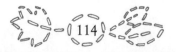

Touchdown!

BBQ Sloppy Joes

Faye Mayberry
Saint David, AZ

*The barbecued beans give this recipe such a unique flavor.
We like to eat these sandwiches with corn chips tucked inside
for a little crunch in every bite.*

1 lb. ground beef
1/2 onion, chopped
28-oz. can barbecued beans
14-1/2 oz. can stewed tomatoes

1-1/2 oz. pkg. Sloppy Joe mix
6 sandwich buns, split and
   toasted

Brown beef and onion in a skillet over medium heat; drain. Stir in remaining ingredients except buns; simmer for about 30 minutes. Serve over toasted buns. Serve 6.

Tex-Mex Burgers

Kay Simpson
Clovis, CA

*A great twist on the Mexican food that is so popular here in California...
my 10-year-old even loves them! You will love the terrific flavor
and the quick prep time of this recipe.*

2 lbs. ground beef
1 c. shredded Cheddar cheese
1/2 c. onion, grated
1/2 c. salsa

2 to 3 cups tortilla chips,
   crushed
8 sandwich buns, split

Combine all ingredients in a bowl except buns; shape into patties. Grill over medium heat to desired doneness. Serve on buns. Makes 8 burgers.

Chocolate Oatmeal Bars

Renee Johnson
Smithville, TN

These are great for tailgating!

1 c. butter, softened
2 c. dark brown sugar, packed
2 eggs, beaten
1 T. vanilla extract
2-1/2 c. all-purpose flour

1 t. salt
1 t. baking soda
3 c. quick-cooking oats,
    uncooked
1 c. chopped pecans

Blend together butter and brown sugar in a large bowl. Add eggs and vanilla; beat well. Stir in flour, salt and baking soda. Add oats; stir to combine. Press 2/3 of oat mixture into a 13"x9" baking pan that has been sprayed with non-stick vegetable spray. Spread evenly with topping; sprinkle with nuts. Drop remaining oat mixture by tablespoonfuls; gently spread over topping. Bake at 350 degrees for 25 to 30 minutes, until golden. Cool completely; slice into bars. Makes 2 dozen.

Topping:

12-oz. pkg. semi-sweet
    chocolate chips
14-oz. can sweetened
    condensed milk

1/4 c. butter
2 t. vanilla extract
1/2 t. salt

Combine chocolate chips, condensed milk, butter, vanilla and salt in a saucepan. Cook over medium heat, stirring constantly, until chocolate has melted.

A vintage lunchbox is just right
for filling with cookies and sweet treats
for snacking on...it's so easy to
take anywhere.

Touchdown!

Frosted Cashew Cookies

Terry Heyndrickx
Morton, IL

Over the years, my grandma's most-loved cookie recipe has been shared with friends & family. When the holiday season started each year, her home would fill up with card tables, as did my mother's. Each table held wonderful baked items and the aroma and warmth from their love of baking and sharing spread throughout many homes in our neighborhood. I now start baking this recipe when the crisp and cool weather of the fall season begins.

1/2 c. butter, softened
1 c. brown sugar, packed
1 egg, beaten
1/2 t. vanilla extract
2 c. all-purpose flour
3/4 t. baking powder

3/4 t. baking soda
1/4 t. salt
1/3 c. sour cream
1-3/4 c. salted whole cashews
Garnish: 42 whole cashews

Blend together butter and sugar until light and fluffy. Beat in egg and vanilla. Stir together dry ingredients; add alternately with sour cream. Mix well. Carefully fold in 1-3/4 cups cashews. Drop by teaspoonfuls onto greased baking sheets. Bake at 400 degrees for 10 minutes, or until lightly golden; cool. Frost cookies; top with remaining cashews. Makes 3-1/2 dozen.

Golden Butter Icing:

1/2 c. butter
1/4 t. vanilla extract

3 T. half-and-half
2 c. powdered sugar

Melt butter in a saucepan over medium heat until beginning to brown. Remove from heat; add half-and-half and vanilla. Stir in powdered sugar; beat until smooth and thick enough to spread.

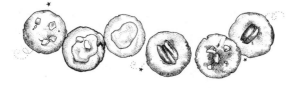

Spicy Pumpkin Cookies

Lynne McKaige
Savage, MN

The aroma of these homebaked cookies makes it almost impossible not to eat them warm right from the oven. If you end up with extra frosting you'll know why!

18-1/2 oz. pkg. yellow cake mix
2 t. pumpkin pie spice
1 c. canned pumpkin
1/4 c. butter, softened

Optional: 1/2 c. raisins
16-oz. container vanilla frosting
nutmeg to taste

In a large bowl, combine cake mix, spice, pumpkin and butter. Beat together with an electric mixer on medium speed until well combined, about 2 minutes. Stir in raisins, if desired. Drop dough by generous tablespoonfuls, 2 inches apart on lightly greased baking sheets. Bake at 375 degrees for 11 to 14 minutes, or until set and lightly golden around edges. Cool for one to 2 minutes; remove to wire rack. Cool completely. Spread with frosting; sprinkle with nutmeg. Makes 2-1/2 dozen.

Double-Chip Bars

Loretta Schneider
Midland, TX

I was raised German Mennonite and guests were frequent in our home. A favorite recipe for 2 generations, these bars were always a quick-to-fix dessert or snack when visitors arrived.

1 c. sugar
1 c. light corn syrup
12-oz. jar crunchy peanut butter
4 c. doughnut-shaped oat cereal

12-oz. pkg. semi-sweet chocolate chips
11-oz. pkg. butterscotch chips

Combine sugar and corn syrup in a saucepan over medium heat; bring to a boil. Cook until sugar is dissolved. Fold in peanut butter; stir well. Stir in cereal; spread into an ungreased 13"x9" baking pan. Melt chocolate chips and butterscotch chips together in a saucepan over medium heat, stirring to blend. Spread over top; slice into squares. Makes 15.

BOO!

Halloween
Tricks & Treats

Frightfully fun dress-up ideas... in a dash!

A straw hat, flannel shirt, bib overalls, a little straw tucked here and there and you're an instant scarecrow.

Dress in black from head to toe, slip on a raincoat and a pair of sunglasses to transform into a secret agent.

How about dressing up as a tourist? Swing a camera around your neck and hold a map...a quick & easy costume!

The fabulous 1950's...a white tee shirt, pair of rolled up jeans, bobby socks, sunglasses and a ponytail!

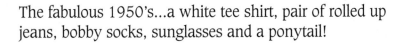

Becoming a black cat has never been so easy...dress in black, use face paint to add a cute cat nose and whiskers, and ears can be made out of cardboard, painted black and held in place with bobby pins.

Spiced Cake Doughnuts

Katherine Nelson
Centerville, UT

These are a must-have Halloween tradition in our home.

1/4 c. shortening	1 t. cinnamon
1 c. sugar	1 t. nutmeg
3 eggs, beaten	1/4 t. mace
1 t. vanilla extract	1/2 c. buttermilk
5 c. all-purpose flour	1 c. apple, peeled, cored
1 T. baking powder	and grated
1 t. baking soda	oil for deep frying
2 t. salt	Garnish: colored sprinkles

Blend together shortening and sugar in a large bowl; beat in eggs and vanilla. In a separate bowl, combine flour, baking powder, baking soda, salt and spices; add to shortening mixture alternately with buttermilk. Fold in apple. Cover and refrigerate for at least 2 hours. On a lightly floured surface, roll dough out to 1/2-inch thick. Cut with a floured 2-1/2 inch doughnut cutter. In an electric skillet or deep fryer, heat oil to 375 degrees. Fry doughnuts, a few at a time, until golden on both sides; drain on paper towels. Frost doughnuts with Brown Sugar Frosting; top with sprinkles. Makes about 2 dozen.

Brown Sugar Frosting:

1/2 c. brown sugar, packed	1/4 c. whipping cream
3 T. butter	1-3/4 c. powdered sugar

Combine brown sugar and butter in a saucepan over medium heat; bring to a boil. Cook and stir for one minute, or until slightly thickened. Pour into a small bowl; let stand for 10 minutes. Add cream; beat until smooth. Gradually add powdered sugar, 1/4 cup at a time, beating well after each addition until frosting achieves desired consistency.

Halloween Muffins

Donna Cook
Hillsborough, NJ

I made these for my son and called them Halloween Muffins. If he knew that apple and pumpkin were in them...I don't think he would have eaten them! I have made them healthier with the addition of egg substitute and applesauce.

2-1/2 c. all-purpose flour
2 c. sugar
1 t. baking soda
1/2 t. salt
1 T. pumpkin pie spice
1/2 c. egg substitute

1 c. canned pumpkin
1/4 c. oil
1/4 c. applesauce
2 c. Granny Smith apples,
    peeled, cored and grated

In a large bowl, whisk together flour, sugar, baking soda, salt and spice; set aside. Combine remaining ingredients in a separate bowl; add to flour mixture. Stir just until moistened. Spoon batter into greased or paper-lined muffin cups, filling 2/3 full. Sprinkle with topping. Bake at 350 degrees for 30 to 35 minutes, until a toothpick comes out clean. Makes 1-1/2 dozen.

Topping:

1/2 c. all-purpose flour
1/2 c. sugar

1/4 c. butter
1/2 t. cinnamon

Use a pastry blender to combine all ingredients until mixture is crumbly.

Dress up the family table with Halloween-inspired tablecloths, placemats, napkins and dishes...they make any meal so much more fun!

Halloween Tricks & Treats

Friendship Pumpkin Bread

Kendra Walker
Hamilton, OH

*Pumpkin bread is a family favorite on Trick-or-Treat Night. Family &
friends come over to our house and we gather in the yard to share
treats with all the goblins, ghosts and superheroes that come to
our neighborhood.*

1/3 c. shortening	3/4 t. salt
1-1/3 c. sugar	1/2 t. nutmeg
2 eggs	1/2 t. cinnamon
1 c. canned pumpkin	1/3 c. water
1-2/3 c. all-purpose flour	1/2 t. vanilla extract
1/4 t. baking powder	1/2 c. chopped walnuts
1 t. baking soda	

Blend together shortening and sugar. Add eggs, one at a time, beating
well after each addition; stir in pumpkin. In a separate bowl, combine
dry ingredients. In a small bowl, mix together water and vanilla. Add
dry ingredients to pumpkin mixture alternately with water mixture,
stirring just until smooth. Stir in nuts. Spread into 2 greased and
floured 9"x5" loaf pans. Bake at 350 degrees for 45 minutes. Cool in
pans for 5 minutes before turning out. Makes 2 loaves.

Use small hors d'oeuvre cutters or a sharp knife
to cut Jack-'O-Lantern faces from slices of
Friendship Pumpkin Bread...clever!

Hot Witches' Brew

Jean Clemmons
Maryville, TN

When we moved to the mountains, we gathered the neighbors on Halloween, made a bonfire behind our home and served this "witches' brew" during our wienie roast.

2 qts. apple cider
1-3/4 c. lemon-lime soda
2 c. orange juice
1 t. cinnamon
1/2 t. allspice

1/4 t. nutmeg
1/4 t. ground cloves
1/4 c. brown sugar, packed
Optional: orange slices,
   24 4-inch cinnamon sticks

Combine cider, soda, orange juice, spices and brown sugar in a large pot over medium heat. Simmer, stirring often, until heated through; ladle into cups. Garnish with orange slices and cinnamon sticks, if desired. Makes 24 servings.

Orange-Amaretto Punch

Kimberly Hancock
Murrieta, CA

This sparkling punch will be a hit!

6-oz. can frozen lemonade
  concentrate, thawed
2 c. water
1-oz. bottle almond extract

1/2 gal. orange sherbet,
  softened
2 2-ltr. bottles ginger ale, chilled
Garnish: 1 orange, sliced

Combine lemonade, water and extract. Stir well; chill until ready to serve. Scoop sherbet into punch bowl. Add lemonade mixture; slowly pour in ginger ale. Stir gently. Garnish with orange slices on top. Serve immediately. Makes 26 servings.

A drop of black food coloring stirred into any punch will make it look really eerie...Halloween-perfect!

Halloween Tricks & Treats

Frightfully Fun Punch

Jolene Roberts
Quincy, IL

This recipe is so easy to prepare and the drink mix can be changed. I was invited to a wedding about a year ago and the bride thought someone else was taking care of the punch. I ran to the store, got the ingredients and all was well!

2 pkgs. orange drink mix
2 c. sugar
2 qts. water

46-oz. can pineapple juice
1 qt. ginger ale, chilled

Mix together drink mix, sugar and water in a large pitcher. Add pineapple juice; chill. Add ginger ale at serving time. Serve immediately. Makes 25 to 30 servings.

Gone batty? Friends will love this centerpiece. Hollow out a pumpkin and slip a block of florists' foam inside. Cut bat shapes from heavy black paper, then tape one bat to the end of a length of black pipe cleaner; repeat for as many bats as desired. Insert the stems into the floral foam and you'll have bats flying in all directions!

Spooky Snack Mix

Jen Lindholm
Winona, MN

Microwave popcorn works great for this recipe. My favorite flavors of jellybeans to use for Halloween are tangerine, root beer, lemon, orange juice, punch, green apple and licorice.

2 c. popped popcorn
1 c. bite-size crispy wheat
  squares
1/2 c. sweetened, dried
  cranberries

1 T. sugar
1 t. cinnamon
2-1/2 c. mini jellybeans
2 c. mini pretzel twists

In a large bowl, combine popcorn, cereal and cranberries; spray with non-stick vegetable spray for 4 to 5 seconds. Combine sugar and cinnamon; toss with popcorn mixture. Stir in jellybeans and pretzels. Store in an airtight container. Makes about 8 cups.

A glowing message...it's so easy to create! Wrap the outsides of glass pillar-candle holders with gold, yellow or brown tissue paper; secure the edges with double-stick tape. Add Halloween greetings by carefully applying stick-on letters, from the scrapbook or office supply store, to each.

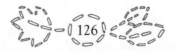

Happy Trails Snack Mix

Mary Ann Dell
Phoenixville, PA

This is a fun treat to share with neighbors.

3 c. mini pretzel twists
2 c. mixed nuts
1 c. crispy corn puff cereal
1 c. dried apple, chopped
1 c. raisins

3/4 c. dried pineapple, chopped
2.1-oz. pkg. candy-coated fruit
chews
1.9-oz. pkg. candy-coated
chocolates

Combine all ingredients in a large bowl; toss to mix well. Store in an airtight container. Makes 2 quarts.

Ghosts, like ladies, never speak till spoke to.

– Richard Harris Barham

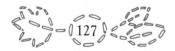

Sneaky Snakes

Wendy Jacobs
Idaho Falls, ID

Mom made these for our Halloween party at school and they were a hit with all the kids...teachers too!

1/3 c. sour cream
1/3 c. thick and chunky salsa
6 soft bread sticks, halved
   lengthwise
8 slices American cheese,
   each cut into 3 strips

Garnish: chopped black olives,
   softened cream cheese, sliced
   pimento, sliced green olives,
   shredded lettuce

Combine sour cream and salsa in a small bowl; spread over cut sides of each bread stick. Place 4 strips cheese onto bottom half of each bread stick; cover with top half. To decorate each snake sandwich, attach 2 pieces chopped black olive to one end of top of sandwich with dot of cream cheese for eyes. Cut a piece of pimento into tongue shape; place it between bread stick halves for a tongue. Attach slices of green olives to the top of sandwich with dot of cream cheese for snakeskin design. Place shredded lettuce onto a platter; set sandwiches onto lettuce. Makes 6 sandwiches.

Everyone loves Halloween party poppers. Fill cardboard tubes with candy and small treats, then wrap each tube in tissue paper, securing the ends with curling ribbon. Dress up the tissue paper with stickers...it's easy!

Tailgate Sandwich Ring, page 113

Deluxe Cocktail Sausages, page 91

Ranch Ham & Tortilla Pinwheels, page 106

Blue-Ribbon Pumpkin Roll, page 139

Apple & Spice Baked French Toast, page 68

Sunrise Skillet, page 67

Friendship Pumpkin Bread, page 123

Mummy Dogs, page 132

Campers' Beans, page 77

Laura's Chicken Pesto Pizza, page 98

Sweet Potato Cornbread, page 160

Beefy Harvest Soup, page 130

Skillet S'mores, page 86

Garlicky Herbed Pork Roast, page 58

Minted Baby Carrots, page 146

Walnut Raisin Pie, page 165

Easy Chili Rellenos, page 49

Old-Fashioned Turkey Pot Pie, page 182

Gwen's Scalloped Corn, page 152

Tangy Turkey Salad Croissants, page 176

Seafood Pinwheels, page 107

French Onion Soup, page 42

Whipped Pumpkin Pie, page 169

B-A-T Sandwich

Amber Baker
Terre Haute, IN

Don't worry...no real bats here! This recipe is good for avocado lovers and is so simple to prepare.

1 avocado, pitted, peeled
   and sliced
salt to taste
4 slices bread, toasted

6 slices bacon, crisply cooked
   and crumbled
1/2 tomato, sliced

Mash avocado until smooth; stir in salt. Spread avocado thickly over 2 pieces of toast. Top with bacon, tomato and remaining bread. Makes 2 sandwiches.

Graveyard Grub

Donna Fisher
Delaware, OH

This monster-size sandwich is so good, we always have to make more than one for our family!

3/4-lb. round focaccia bread,
   halved horizontally
1/2 c. cream cheese with chive
   and onion, softened
8 curly leaf lettuce leaves,
   divided

1/2 lb. deli turkey breast,
   thinly sliced
6 slices American cheese
1/2 lb. deli ham, thinly sliced
6 slices provolone cheese
2 tomatoes, thinly sliced

Spread both cut sides of focaccia bread with cream cheese. Place half the lettuce on bottom half. Layer with turkey, American cheese, ham, provolone cheese, tomatoes and remaining lettuce. Cover with top half of bread. Secure sandwich with a long toothpick; cut into 6 wedges. Makes 6 servings.

Beefy Harvest Soup

Courtesy of
BeefItsWhatsForDinner.com

Other pasta shapes, such as rotini, bowties, medium shells or ditalini, may be substituted for large elbow macaroni; adjust cooking time as needed.

1 lb. lean ground beef
2 c. water
14-1/2 oz. can Italian-style
  stewed tomatoes
1-1/2 c. frozen mixed
  vegetables
4 c. reduced-sodium
  beef broth

1 c. large elbow macaroni,
  uncooked
1/4 lb. smoked beef sausage,
  sliced
salt and pepper to taste

Heat large non-stick skillet over medium heat until hot. Add beef; cook 8 to 10 minutes, breaking into crumbles and stirring occasionally. Remove from skillet with slotted spoon. Remove drippings. Meanwhile, combine water, tomatoes with juice, vegetables and broth in large saucepan; bring to a boil. Stir in macaroni and beef; return to a boil. Reduce heat; simmer, uncovered, 8 minutes, stirring occasionally. Stir in sausage; continue simmering 2 to 4 minutes, or until macaroni is tender and beef sausage is cooked through. Season with salt and pepper, as desired. Serves 5.

For a centerpiece in seconds,
place a witch hat on a plump pumpkin!

Halloween Tricks & Treats

Devilishly Delightful Spaghetti

Stephanie White
Sapulpa, OK

This is our favorite Halloween night recipe...it's so easy just to add all of the ingredients into the slow cooker. I start this recipe in the afternoon and go about finishing all of the last-minute costume touch-ups. When we are finished trick-or-treating around the neighborhood, we have a nice warm meal waiting for us at home.

1 lb. ground beef, browned
   and drained
1-1/4 oz. pkg. spaghetti sauce
   mix
2 T. onion, minced
1 T. garlic, minced

8-oz. can tomato sauce
4-1/2 c. tomato juice
4-oz. can mushroom stems
   and pieces, drained
8-oz. pkg. spaghetti, uncooked
salt and pepper to taste

Combine all ingredients except spaghetti in a slow cooker. Cover and cook on low setting for 6 to 8 hours. Add half of the spaghetti, coarsely broken, reserving remaining spaghetti for another use. Turn on high setting and cook until spaghetti is tender, about one hour. Sprinkle with salt and pepper. Serves 6.

Give any sandwich a goblin face...kids (and adults too!) will love 'em! Arrange olive slices for eyes, a banana pepper nose, carrot crinkle ears and parsley hair.

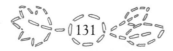

Super Sausage Bread

Tracy Evans
Leesburg, OH

I make this recipe when my family gets together for our annual Halloween party. We keep the tradition of meeting for every single holiday even though there are enough of us to fill a gymnasium!

11-oz. tube refrigerated French
   bread dough
1/2 lb. ground pork sausage,
   browned and drained

1 c. shredded Cheddar cheese
Optional: pizza sauce, warmed

Roll out dough into a 12-inch circle. Spoon sausage down center; sprinkle with cheese. Fold over sides and ends; pinch together to seal. Place on an ungreased baking sheet. Bake at 350 degrees for 30 to 35 minutes. Cool for 30 minutes; slice into 12 pieces. Serve with warm pizza sauce for dipping, if desired. Makes 12 servings.

Mummy Dogs

Sophia Graves
Okeechobee, FL

When Hurricane Wilma disrupted our town's trick-or-treating in 2005, I decided to have an impromptu Halloween get-together...these were the hit of the party!

8-oz. tube refrigerated
   crescent rolls

10 hot dogs
Garnish: mustard

Separate rolls at perforations creating 4 rectangles; press together perforations. Cut each rectangle lengthwise into 10 strips. Wrap 4 strips around each hot dog; leave a space open for "face." Place on an ungreased baking sheet; spray dough lightly with non-stick vegetable spray. Bake at 375 degrees for 13 to 17 minutes, until dough is light golden. Draw on eyes and mouth with mustard. Makes 10 servings.

Halloween Tricks & Treats

Monster Toes & Goop

Angie Venable
Ostrander, OH

These saucy, spicy wings will disappear like magic...and don't fear,
the "Goop" is only a tangy dipping sauce!

3-1/2 lbs. chicken wings
1/2 c. soy sauce
2 t. fresh ginger, peeled and
   grated

1/4 t. red pepper flakes
1 t. Chinese 5-spice powder
2 cloves garlic, minced

Place wings in a large plastic zipping bag; set in a shallow dish.
Mix together remaining ingredients; pour over wings. Toss to coat.
Refrigerate for 6 hours to overnight, turning bag occasionally. Remove
wings from bag, reserving marinade. Arrange on an aluminum foil-
lined 15"x10" jelly-roll pan. Bake at 450 degrees for 10 minutes.
Brush with reserved marinade; discard any remaining marinade. Bake
for an additional 15 to 20 minutes, until chicken is golden and tender.
Serve with Goop. Makes about 20.

Goop:

8-oz. container sour cream
3 T. coarse mustard

Garnish: chopped fresh chives

Stir together sour cream and mustard; garnish with chives.

Store-bought chicken fingers easily become monster claws...
arrange several on a plate, then add red peppers
cut into triangle shapes for the "nails!"

Halloween Scares

Sue Workman
Dutton, MT

When I was a little girl, my mother was always up for fun, especially at Halloween. She would come up with great recipes and fun tricks for our neighborhood as well as treats. This is one surprise main dish she made for Halloween dinner before I went out to gather treats and avoid tricks!

6 boneless, skinless chicken
   breasts
3 eggs, beaten
1/2 c. milk
1/2 t. salt

1/4 t. pepper
2 c. Italian-style dry bread
   crumbs
1/4 c. butter, melted
Garnish: lettuce

Partially cut chicken breasts to create 4 "fingers" and a "thumb;" the uncut part of the breast will be the palm of the "hand." Whisk together eggs, milk, salt and pepper in a shallow bowl. Dredge chicken in egg mixture; coat with bread crumbs. Melt butter in a large skillet over medium heat. Add chicken; cook until golden. Arrange on baking sheets. Bake at 350 degrees for 10 to 15 minutes, until cooked through. Place chicken breast "hands" on a lettuce leaf to give the appearance of a curved hand. Serves 6.

Spooky tortilla chips are so easy to make! Spray a baking sheet with non-stick vegetable spray; set aside. Cut flour tortillas with Halloween-shaped cookie cutters; lightly spray each cut-out with vegetable spray. Place on baking sheet, sprinkle with salt and bake at 350 degrees for 5 to 7 minutes.

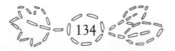

Bewitching Baked Chicken Salad

Vickie
Gooseberry Patch

*I made this for our **Gooseberry Patch** Halloween potluck...*
we had such a great time!

6 to 8 boneless, skinless
   chicken breasts, halved
1 to 2 T. olive oil
kosher salt to taste
1 c. mayonnaise
4 c. celery, sliced
1/2 c. onion, chopped

8-oz. pkg. shredded sharp
   Cheddar cheese, divided
2 T. lemon juice
1 c. slivered almonds, toasted
salt and pepper to taste
2 c. kettle-style potato chips,
   crushed

Brush chicken with oil; sprinkle with kosher salt. Arrange in a
lightly greased 13"x9" baking pan. Bake at 350 degrees for 45 to
50 minutes. Let cool; cube to equal about 6 cups chicken. Combine
with remaining ingredients except chips; toss lightly. Place in a
lightly greased 13"x9" baking pan. Bake at 350 degrees for 30 to
35 minutes, until hot and bubbly. Combine remaining cheese and
potato chips; sprinkle over casserole. Return to oven until cheese
melts, about 10 minutes. Serve warm. Makes 8 to 10 servings.

Chicken & Apple Patties

Veronica Gideon
Sarasota, FL

We have this for dinner when we come home from the pumpkin patch.

2 T. olive oil
1 red apple, peeled, cored,
   and chopped

1 red onion, chopped
1 lb. ground chicken
2 T. poultry seasoning

Heat oil in a skillet over medium heat; sauté apple and onion until
tender. Cool slightly. In a large bowl, combine chicken, seasoning
and apple mixture. Shape into 4 patties. Fry in a greased skillet over
medium heat for 4 minutes per side. Serves 4.

Halloween Tarantulas

Stacie Avner
Delaware, OH

*I made these treats for my son's class on his birthday since
it falls just before Halloween.*

2 c. all-purpose flour
1/2 t. baking powder
1/8 t. baking soda
1/2 t. salt
10 T. butter, softened
1/2 c. brown sugar, packed
1/4 c. sugar
1 egg, beaten

1 t. vanilla extract
2 T. baking cocoa
8-oz. pkg. pretzel sticks
12-oz. pkg. milk chocolate chips
2 T. oil
4 to 6 3-1/4 oz. bottles
   chocolate sprinkles
1/2 c. red cinnamon candies

Combine flour, baking powder, baking soda and salt in a large bowl;
set aside. In a separate bowl, beat together butter and sugars until
light and fluffy. Add egg and vanilla; beat until well blended.
Gradually add flour mixture and baking cocoa; beat until smooth.
Roll dough by tablespoonfuls into balls; place on ungreased baking
sheets. Insert 8 pretzel sticks around each ball for spider "legs."
Bake at 350 degrees until cookies start to turn golden, about 7 to
10 minutes. Cool on wire racks set over wax paper. In a double boiler,
melt chocolate chips with oil. Spread melted chocolate over each cookie;
coat thickly with chocolate sprinkles. Press in 2 red candies for "eyes."
Makes 2-1/2 dozen.

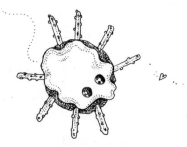

Double, double toil and trouble; fire burn and cauldron bubble.

– Shakespeare's Macbeth

*Halloween*Tricks & Treats

Tricky Treats

Patricia Wissler
Harrisburg, PA

*Every year at church we have Trick-or-Treat and a Halloween party
for the kids. These treats are always a hit with the kids
as well as the adults.*

1/2 c. butter
9 c. mini marshmallows
10 c. crispy rice cereal
1 c. candy corn
1 c. Indian candy corn

3/4 c. mini semi-sweet chocolate
  chips
2 drops yellow food coloring
1 drop red food coloring
20 candy pumpkins

Melt together butter and marshmallows in a large saucepan over
medium heat; stir until smooth. In a large bowl, combine cereal, candy
corn and chocolate chips. Blend food coloring into marshmallow
mixture, adding more coloring if necessary to reach desired shade
of orange. Add marshmallow mixture to cereal mixture; stir quickly
to combine. Spread in a buttered 13"x9" baking pan; press with
buttered hands. While still warm, press on candy pumpkins spaced
1-1/2 to 2 inches apart. Refrigerate for one hour, or until firm; cut
into squares. To make thinner treats, use a 15"x10" jelly-roll pan.
Makes 1-1/2 to 2 dozen.

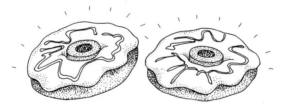

Whip up some Monster Eyes...they're ready in no time!
Spread cream cheese evenly over toasted bagels, leaving
the center holes open, then place an olive slice over the hole.
Squeeze a little catsup over the cream cheese to give
the monster "bloodshot eyes."

Spider Cakes

Sue Workman
Dutton, MT

*My children came up with this recipe when they decided spiders
were the greatest...probably around the time they figured out
that Mom didn't like spiders!*

36 to 48 small pretzel sticks   12 red cinnamon candies
6-inch "snowball" cakes

Press 6 to 8 pretzel sticks into each cake to resemble legs. Place 2 red
candies on cake for eyes. Makes 6.

Salted Nut Rolls

Marcy Richardson
Robbinsdale, MN

This is a family favorite on Halloween.

16-oz. jar dry-roasted peanuts,   14-oz. can sweetened
  divided   condensed milk
1/4 c. butter   10-1/2 oz. pkg. mini
10-oz. pkg. peanut butter chips   marshmallows

Spread half of peanuts in a greased 13"x9" baking pan. Combine
butter, peanut butter chips and condensed milk in a saucepan over
medium heat; stir until melted. Stir in marshmallows until melted;
spread over peanuts. Sprinkle remaining peanuts over top; gently pat
down. Cool; refrigerate until set, about one hour. Slice into squares.
Makes 2 dozen.

Eat, drink and be scary!

– Unknown

Halloween Tricks & Treats

Blue-Ribbon Pumpkin Roll

Laurie Ellithorpe
Argyle, NY

This yummy recipe is blue-ribbon good!

3 eggs, beaten
1 c. sugar
2/3 c. canned pumpkin
3/4 c. all-purpose flour
1 t. baking soda
1 t. cinnamon

1 c. plus 3 T. powdered sugar,
   divided
8-oz. pkg. cream cheese,
   softened
1 t. vanilla extract

Blend together eggs, sugar and pumpkin. In a separate bowl, combine flour, baking soda and cinnamon; fold into pumpkin mixture. Line a 15"x10" jelly-roll pan with parchment paper. Grease and flour the paper; spread batter into pan. Bake at 350 degrees for 15 minutes. Sprinkle 3 tablespoons powdered sugar on a tea towel; turn out warm cake onto towel. Carefully peel off parchment paper. Starting at narrow end, roll up cake and towel together; cool completely on a wire rack, seam-side down. Blend together cream cheese, remaining powdered sugar and vanilla until smooth. Unroll cake; spread with cream cheese mixture and re-roll, removing towel as you roll. Place on a serving plate, seam-side down; cover and chill for at least 2 hours. Serves 10 to 12.

Give pumpkins a glittering sparkle...it's so easy. Lightly coat the outside of a pumpkin with spray adhesive and dust with fine glitter; set aside to dry. If time is short, use a paintbrush to apply white glue to the stem only, then dust it with glitter... try using purple or lime green.

Halloween Gobble-Up Cookies

Carla Vanatta
Sycamore, IL

*I discovered this cookie recipe in a church cookbook...it's been
a family favorite ever since. You can increase the flour
by 1/2 cup if you like a firmer cookie.*

1 c. butter, softened
1 c. brown sugar, packed
1 c. sugar
2 eggs, beaten
1 t. vanilla extract
2-1/2 c. all-purpose flour
1/2 t. salt

1 t. baking powder
1 t. baking soda
2 c. quick-cooking oats,
   uncooked
2 c. lightly toasted rice cereal
1 c. semi-sweet chocolate chips
1 c. chopped walnuts

Combine butter and sugars; beat in eggs and vanilla. In a separate
bowl, combine flour, salt, baking powder and baking soda; gradually
add to butter mixture. Stir in remaining ingredients. Drop by
tablespoonfuls onto greased baking sheets. Bake at 350 degrees
for 9 to 10 minutes. Remove from oven; let stand on baking sheets
for 4 to 5 minutes. Cool on wire rack. Makes 4 to 5 dozen.

Stir up some Grizzly Gorp for snacking...just toss together
2 cups bear-shaped graham crackers, 1 cup mini marshmallows,
1 cup peanuts and ½ cup seedless raisins. Yum!

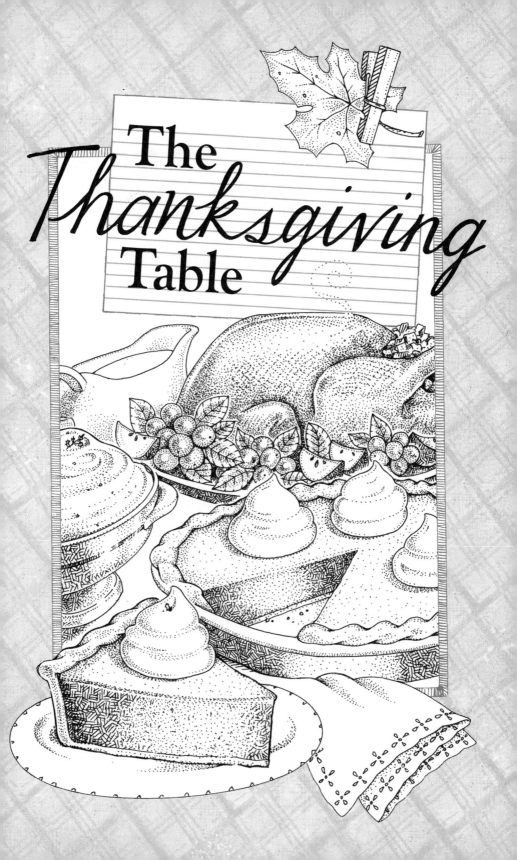

The *Thanksgiving* Table

Turkey Day Tips

Turkey defrosting: Always defrost a frozen turkey in its plastic wrapper, keep it in the refrigerator following these guidelines:

10 to 12 pounds: 2 days   14 to 18 pounds: 4 days
12 to 14 pounds: 3 days   18+ pounds: 5 days

Basting: When it comes to basting, butter's best...nothing beats it for flavor and richness!

Is it done yet? Insert a meat thermometer into the thigh, but not touching bone...it should read 165 degrees.

Heavenly mashed potatoes:
The best way to mash potatoes is to use a potato ricer or food mill... they will come out light, fluffy and oh-so creamy!

Perfect gravy: Add equal amounts of flour and butter to a saucepan over medium heat; blend into a paste. Gradually add enough broth to make a gravy as thick or thin as you like...continue to stir, adding more broth as the gravy thickens. Season with salt and pepper to taste.

The *Thanksgiving* Table

The Perfect Turkey

Nancy Girard
Chesapeake, VA

*We make two turkeys every Thanksgiving...one in the smoker and one
in the oven. This is the recipe that I make most often. It is delicious!
I never stuff my turkeys, I bake my stuffing separately, and always
use real butter.*

10 to 12 lb. turkey, thawed
   if frozen
2 onions, quartered
4 shallots, quartered
1 bulb garlic
1 bunch fresh thyme

1 bunch fresh sage
1 c. white wine or chicken broth
2 T. butter, melted
2-1/2 t. kosher salt
1/2 t. pepper

Pat turkey dry with paper towels. Remove neck and giblets; reserve
for another recipe. Arrange vegetables and herbs in an ungreased
large roasting pan; place turkey on top. Drizzle with wine or broth.
Brush turkey with butter; sprinkle with salt and pepper. Roast at
325 degrees for 1 to 1-1/2 hours, until skin is golden. Tent breast
loosely with aluminum foil. Roast for an additional 1-1/2 to 2 hours,
or until a meat thermometer inserted into thickest part of inner thigh
registers 165 degrees. Transfer turkey to a serving platter. Cover loosely
and let stand for 15 to 20 minutes before carving. Serves 10 to 14.

Clever placecards...childhood
photos at each place setting.
Not only do they bring sweet
memories, but it's fun
to guess who's who!

The Creamiest Mashed Potatoes

Verona Haught
Londonderry, NH

My family really loves mashed potatoes, especially when they are freshly harvested in the autumn. This recipe is ideal to serve alongside the Thanksgiving turkey!

5 to 6 potatoes, peeled and cut
    into 1-inch cubes
3-oz. pkg. cream cheese, thinly
    sliced and softened
3 T. butter, softened
4 to 5 T. half-and-half or milk

2 cloves garlic, minced
salt and pepper to taste
2 T. fresh chives, snipped,
    or 3 T. dried chives
Garnish: additional butter

Cover potatoes with water in a large stockpot over medium-high heat. Boil potatoes until tender when pierced with a fork, about 15 minutes once they begin to boil. Drain; mash with either a hand masher or an electric mixer on medium speed. Add cream cheese, butter, half-and-half or milk, garlic, salt and pepper. Mix well until butter and cream cheese are melted. Fold in chives; top with a dollop or two of butter. Serves 6.

Excellent potatoes, smoking hot, and accompanied by melted butter of the first quality, would alone stamp merit on any dinner.

– Thomas Walker

The *Thanksgiving* Table

New England Wild Rice & Apples
Stefanie St. Pierre
Chatham, MA

A wonderful complement to turkey or chicken, it can also be used as stuffing.

2 T. onion, minced
1/2 c. butter, melted and divided
2 4-oz. pkgs. wild rice, cooked
1 Granny Smith apple, cored, peeled and chopped
1 McIntosh apple, cored and chopped

1 c. bread crumbs
1/2 c. chopped walnuts
1/4 c. orange juice
zest of one orange, chopped

Lightly sauté onion in 3 tablespoons butter. Combine onion and remaining butter with remaining ingredients. Mix well; transfer to a greased 2-quart casserole dish. Cover and bake at 325 degrees for 35 minutes, until apples are tender. Serves 4.

Set out a few little goodies to nibble on while waiting for the turkey to cook. A hollowed-out round loaf of sourdough is perfect filled with all kinds of delicious olives, while other loaves can be filled with cheesy spreads for sampling.

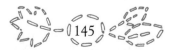

Minted Baby Carrots

Tori Willis
Champaign, IL

I make this wonderful, easy side to complement special-occasion meals or to jazz up a weeknight meal. It's so easy, yet so delicious, and everyone asks for this recipe!

1/2 lb. baby carrots	1 T. lemon zest, minced
1 T. butter	1 T. brown sugar, packed
salt and pepper to taste	2 t. fresh mint, minced

In a stockpot of boiling water, cook carrots 5 minutes. Remove from heat, and drain. Melt butter in a skillet over medium-high heat. Stir in carrots; cook until crisp-tender. Season with salt and pepper to taste. Combine remaining ingredients, and sprinkle over individual servings. Serves 4.

A string of colorful apples, clementines, pears and autumn leaves creates a harvest welcome when hanging across a porch or doorway. Pierce holes in a variety of fruit, then string with twine...a rug-hooking needle is perfect for this. Tie on lots of fresh fall leaves using florists' wire, and hang. Once the season is over, be sure to share the fruit with the birds...they'll love the treat!

The *Thanksgiving* Table

Caramelized Brussels Sprouts

Beth Schlieper
Lakewood, CO

These go great with a golden turkey and all the trimmings. My friend Lisa and I usually eat any leftovers before we can put them away!

4 lbs. Brussels sprouts, trimmed
1/2 c. butter
4 onions, cut into strips
1/4 c. red wine vinegar, divided

2 T. sugar
salt and pepper to taste
Optional: 1/2 c. pistachio nuts, chopped

Steam Brussels sprouts for 8 to 10 minutes, or until just tender-crisp. Melt butter in a deep skillet. Add onions and 3 tablespoons vinegar; cook until golden. Add Brussels sprouts, sugar and remaining vinegar. Sauté over medium heat until sprouts are lightly caramelized. Sprinkle with salt, pepper and nuts, if desired. Serves 8.

Cheesy Green Beans

Roseann Floura
Rockwall, TX

My mother-in-law Jeanette Allen created this recipe. It's a wonderful change-of-pace dish, and I submit it in her memory.

3 T. butter
1/4 c. onion, finely chopped
3 T. all-purpose flour
1 c. milk
12-oz. pkg. American cheese slices, chopped
1/2 t. mustard

1/4 t. Worcestershire sauce
1/8 t. cayenne pepper
6 slices bacon, crisply cooked and crumbled
2 14-1/2 oz. cans French-style green beans, drained

Melt butter in a large saucepan; add onion and cook until transparent. Add flour and stir until absorbed; gradually stir in milk. Cook over medium heat, stirring constantly, until thickened. Stir in cheese until melted. Add remaining ingredients; pour into a lightly greased 1-1/2 quart casserole dish. Bake, uncovered, at 350 degrees until bubbly and golden, about 20 minutes. Serves 6.

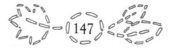

Ham Delight

Connie Hilty
Pearland, TX

A fresh-tasting side for your Thanksgiving table.

2 T. butter
2-1/2 c. cooked ham, cubed
2 green onions, chopped
1 c. pineapple chunks, drained
1/3 c. pineapple juice

4 t. cider vinegar
2 T. brown sugar, packed
2 t. mustard
2 T. cornstarch

Melt butter in a large skillet over medium heat. Sauté ham, onions and pineapple for 5 minutes. Combine remaining ingredients in a small bowl; mix well. Pour over ham mixture; cook until thickened and heated through, about 5 minutes. Serves 4.

Don't forget to fill summertime windowboxes, sap buckets, even watering cans with a burst of autumn! Overflowing with Indian corn, yarrow, mini pumpkins, gourds, leaves and hedge apples, they really take on a harvest feel.

The *Thanksgiving* Table

Sausage-Apple-Pecan Stuffing

Gina McClenning
Valrico, FL

*This recipe for stuffing has been in my family since I was a little girl.
It's an old-fashioned New England-type of stuffing
and is absolutely delicious.*

2 c. onions, chopped
1 c. celery with leaves, chopped
1 c. butter, divided
2 c. chicken broth
14-oz. pkg. plus 6-oz. pkg.
  herb-flavored stuffing mix
16-oz. pkg. ground pork
  sausage, browned and
  drained

3 red apples, cored and chopped
1 c. golden raisins
1/2 c. chopped pecans
2 envs. chicken instant
  seasoning & broth
1 t. cinnamon
salt and pepper to taste

Sauté onions and celery in 1/2 cup butter until onions are golden.
Heat broth in a saucepan over medium heat. Add remaining butter;
cook until melted and set aside. In a large bowl, combine stuffing mix,
onion mixture, sausage, apples, raisins, nuts, instant seasoning and
cinnamon. Blend with your hands, adding broth mixture one cup at
a time until desired consistency is reached. Sprinkle with salt and
pepper. Use to stuff a 16 to 20-pound turkey, or spoon into a buttered
13"x9" baking pan. Cover and bake at 350 degrees for 30 minutes.
Uncover and bake until stuffing is golden and heated through,
20 to 25 minutes more. Serves 8 to 10.

Spiced Peaches

Kimberley Bercaw
Ewa Beach, HI

This has been a family favorite for over 30 years. Our Thanksgiving dinners wouldn't be complete without spiced peaches! This recipe needs to be made at least four days ahead, which is always welcome when planning our Thanksgiving feast.

4 16-oz. cans sliced peaches
   in syrup
2 c. sugar
1 c. cider vinegar

4 4-inch cinnamon sticks
2 t. whole allspice
2 t. ground cloves

Combine all ingredients in a large saucepan over medium heat; bring to a boil. Reduce heat and simmer, uncovered, for 30 minutes until liquid is slightly thickened. Let cool; pour into a covered container. Refrigerate for at least 4 days prior to serving. Remove from refrigerator approximately one hour before serving. Serves 8.

Hang a garland inside this Thanksgiving...snip photos of
family, friends, pets, anything you're thankful for.
Clipped to a ribbon with mini clothespins, they're
a heartfelt reminder to count your blessings.

The *Thanksgiving* Table

Mom's Caramel Sweet Potatoes

Jennifer Mathis
Tupelo, MS

This is the best sweet potato casserole you'll ever have! Sweet and creamy...a must-have on the holiday table. My entire family has enjoyed this for years.

6 sweet potatoes, peeled
   and cubed
1/2 c. brown sugar, packed
1 c. butter, sliced and divided

1 t. vanilla extract
1/2 t. imitation butter flavoring
1 c. sugar
1 c. half-and-half

In a large saucepan, cover sweet potatoes with water. Bring to a boil over medium-high heat. Cook until fork-tender; drain. With an electric mixer on medium speed, beat until smooth. Add brown sugar, 1/2 cup butter, vanilla and butter flavoring to sweet potatoes; mix well. Pour into a buttered large serving bowl; make a well in center for sauce. Keep warm until caramel sauce is added. To make the caramel sauce, combine sugar, half-and-half and remaining butter in a large skillet. Cook over medium-low heat for 20 to 25 minutes, until honey-colored and slightly thickened. Pour sauce into well in sweet potatoes. Serves 8 to 10.

Count your many blessings, every doubt will fly,
And you will keep singing as the days go by.

– John Oatman, Jr.

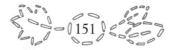

Garlic Mashed Potatoes

Judi Towner
Clarks Summit, PA

*A potato recipe passed down in my family. This delicious side dish is
a big hit at Thanksgiving and is loved by children as well as adults.*

5 lbs. potatoes, peeled and
   quartered
2 t. garlic, minced
1/2 t. salt
1/4 c. butter, softened
1 c. sour cream

1/2 c. cream cheese, softened
1 T. Italian salad dressing mix
1 t. onion salt
1/2 t. pepper
1/4 c. milk

Cover potatoes with water in a large saucepan; add garlic and salt.
Cook over medium heat until tender; drain well. Add remaining
ingredients. With an electric mixer on medium speed, beat until
mixture is smooth. Serve immediately. Serves 8 to 10.

Gwen's Scalloped Corn

Tobie Patton
Springfield, OH

*I was given this recipe by my best friend's mother, Gwen. I am
always asked to make this dish at every family dinner as it's
so moist and delicious...and very easy to prepare.*

15-oz. can corn, drained
15-oz. can creamed corn
1/2 c. butter, melted
8-oz. container sour cream

8-1/2 oz. pkg. corn muffin mix
dried parsley, salt and pepper
   to taste

Combine all ingredients in a medium bowl; mix well. Spray a
9"x9" baking pan with non-stick vegetable spray. Spread corn
mixture evenly in pan. Bake, uncovered, at 350 degrees for
30 minutes, or until golden. Let stand for 10 minutes before
serving. Makes 6 servings.

The *Thanksgiving* Table

Harvest Vegetables

Jo Ann
Gooseberry Patch

Roasted and slightly garlicky in flavor, these vegetables are always on the family table during the holidays.

2 lbs. butternut squash, halved,
   seeded and cut into
   1-1/2 inch cubes
2 lbs. new redskin potatoes,
   quartered
2 to 3 red onions, quartered

16-oz. pkg. baby carrots
4 to 6 cloves garlic, crushed
3 T. olive oil, divided
2 t. coarse salt, divided
1/4 t. pepper, divided

Combine vegetables and garlic; spread evenly onto 2 lightly greased baking sheets. Toss with oil, salt and pepper. Bake at 450 degrees for 40 to 50 minutes, tossing vegetables and rotating sheets from top to bottom of oven halfway through. Serve hot or at room temperature. Makes 8 servings.

Serve savory baked mini pumpkins this year...they're so simple!
Cut the tops off pumpkins and hollow out, removing all
seeds. Brush the insides with olive oil; season with
salt & pepper. Add a sprinkle of Parmesan cheese inside,
replace the tops and bake at 350 degrees for 40 minutes.

Mimi's Oyster Dressing

Teresa Potter
Branson, MO

This recipe has been handed down from my grandmother to my mother and the rest of the family. It was unwritten so when I had my first Thanksgiving dinner, Mother came over to help with the dressing. It has been a Thanksgiving and Christmas tradition for over 60 years.

3 loaves sliced bread
48-oz. plus 14-oz. containers
    chicken broth, divided
turkey neck and gizzards
2 to 3 c. celery, chopped

1 onion, chopped
1/2-oz. jar ground sage
2 to 3 8-oz. cans oysters,
    drained

About 3 days in advance, lay bread out in a single layer to dry. When dry, tear into bread crumbs and place into 2 very large bowls; set aside. Drain enough broth from roast turkey, or if not roasting a turkey, use enough chicken broth, to fill a large saucepan 3/4 full. Add neck and gizzards and bring to a boil; simmer 30 minutes. Remove neck and gizzards; discard, or if desired, chop gizzards and meat from neck and return to saucepan. Add celery, onion and sage to broth. Simmer 30 minutes. Spoon oysters over bread crumbs. Pour broth mixture over bread crumbs and begin mixing gently. Add as much additional chicken broth as needed to make bread crumbs very moist, but still hold together. Spoon into a lightly greased large aluminum foil baking pan; cover with aluminum foil. Bake at 350 degrees for 40 minutes; uncover and continue baking an additional 20 minutes. Makes 12 to 18 servings.

Keep holiday silver shining for Thanksgiving Day! Arrange silver pieces in an aluminum foil-lined pan, add one teaspoonful baking soda and salt; fill with water. Soak silver until shiny, then dry thoroughly.

The *Thanksgiving* Table

Grandma Westfall's Rolls

Bev Westfall
Berlin, NY

*It just wouldn't be Thanksgiving or Christmas without these rolls...
they're treated like gold! We usually make four times the recipe.*

1 c. milk
1 env. active dry yeast
1/4 c. sugar
3 T. shortening

1 t. salt
1 egg, beaten
3-1/2 c. all-purpose flour

Heat milk just to boiling, about 110 to 115 degrees; remove from
heat. Pour milk over yeast, sugar, shortening and salt in a large
bowl. Add egg and mix well. Gradually stir in flour; place dough in a
second, greased bowl. Let rise for one hour; punch down. Form into
walnut-size balls or smaller; place 3 balls in each greased muffin
cup. Cover and let rise until double in size, about 2 hours. Bake at
425 degrees for 6 minutes, or until golden. Makes 2 dozen.

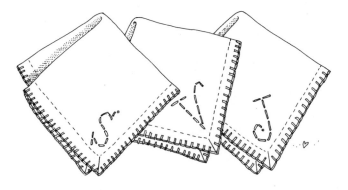

Add a sweet touch to plain cloth napkins. Use a simple
straight embroidery stitch to add a guest's initial to each
napkin, then finish off the edges with a blanket stitch.

Family-Style Chicken Dumplings

Trudy Gernert
Seymour, IN

My sister always makes these for Thanksgiving...easy and delicious.

3 14-1/2 oz. cans chicken broth
1/2 t. dried sage
1 t. dried rosemary
1 whole onion
2 carrots, peeled and diced

2 stalks celery, diced
1/2 t. pepper
12-oz. tube refrigerated biscuits,
    quartered

Bring broth to a boil in a Dutch oven over medium heat. Add remaining ingredients except biscuits. Simmer for 10 minutes; remove onion and return to a boil. Add biscuits; stir. Simmer for about 30 minutes, until biscuits are set. Makes 10 servings.

A creative, natural place-setting idea. Remove top petals and center of an artichoke. Squeeze a few drops of lemon juice into the core to prevent browning, then insert a glass votive and candle.

Mom's Dressing

Samantha Moyer
Farragut, IA

My mom is the only one ever asked to make dressing for the family's holiday dinners. She usually makes two pans, one plain and one with oysters. Either way, it is always a hit.

16-oz. pkg. unseasoned
  bread cubes
1-1/2 t. dried sage
1 t. salt
1/2 t. pepper

1 c. onion, chopped
1 c. celery, diced
6 T. butter
4 to 4-1/2 c. chicken broth
5 eggs, beaten

Toss bread cubes with sage, salt and pepper; set aside. Sauté onion and celery in butter over medium heat. Combine bread with onion mixture in a large bowl. Slowly add 4 cups broth and let stand until broth is absorbed. Add more broth if needed; mixture should be very soft. Fold eggs into bread mixture; stir gently, just until combined. Spread in a 13"x9" baking pan that has been sprayed with non-stick vegetable spray. Bake, covered, at 350 degrees for one hour, then uncover and bake 15 minutes longer. Serves 6 to 8.

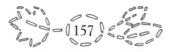

Farmhouse Ham

Brenda Smith
Delaware, OH

Our family always heads back home to the farm for the holidays. It's great to see all the little ones running around, while my sisters and I talk, laugh and help prepare dinner together. This ham and special sauce is one we've always served...it just can't be beat.

3 to 4-lb. fully-cooked boneless
   ham, halved
1/2 c. apple jelly
2 t. mustard

2/3 c. ginger ale, divided
21-oz. can cherry pie filling
2 T. cornstarch

With a knife, score surface of ham into diamond shapes, about 1/2 inch deep. In a small bowl, combine jelly, mustard and one tablespoon ginger ale; rub over ham. Place ham halves in a slow cooker. Cover and cook on low setting for 4 to 5 hours, or until a meat thermometer reads 140 degrees and ham is heated through. Baste with cooking juices toward end of cooking time. For sauce, place pie filling in a saucepan over medium heat. Combine cornstarch and remaining ginger ale; stir into pie filling until blended. Bring to a boil; cook and stir for 2 minutes, or until thickened. Serve over ham. Serves 10 to 12.

For each new morning with its light,
For rest and shelter of the night,
For health and food, for love and friends,
For everything Thy goodness sends.

– Ralph Waldo Emerson

The *Thanksgiving* Table

Mom's Cranberry Salad

Beverly Ray
Brandon, FL

This recipe was passed down from my husband's Grandma Whitehill to my mother-in-law, and now I have been making it for 40 years.

3-oz. pkg. lemon gelatin mix
3-oz. pkg. raspberry gelatin mix
2 c. boiling water
14-1/2 oz. can whole-berry
   cranberry sauce

8-oz. can crushed pineapple,
   drained
1/2 c. chopped pecans

Dissolve gelatin mixes in boiling water; add cranberry sauce, pineapple and nuts. Stir until well blended. Pour into an 8"x8" baking pan; chill for 3 to 4 hours, or overnight. Makes 9 to 12 servings.

Cranberry-Jalapeño Relish

Shona Macan
Loveland, CO

I found this recipe in an old newspaper clipping...a tasty change from traditional cranberry relish. Remember to make a day ahead to allow the flavors to blend.

1 c. sugar
1 c. water
12-oz. pkg. cranberries
2 jalapeños, seeded and minced

1 T. fresh cilantro, chopped
1/2 t. ground cumin
2 to 3 green onions, sliced
1 T. lime juice

Combine sugar and water in a saucepan over medium heat; bring to a boil. Add cranberries; return to a boil. Cook for 10 minutes without stirring. Pour into a bowl and allow to cool. Add remaining ingredients; mix gently. Refrigerate. Serve chilled or at room temperature. Makes 8 servings.

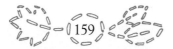

Sweet Potato Cornbread

Jessica Whitfield
Rocky Face, GA

This rich cornbread is sure to become your family favorite. Baking it
in a skillet makes the edges so wonderfully golden brown.
Serve it with honey butter or raspberry jam.

2 c. self-rising cornmeal mix
1/4 c. sugar
1 t. cinnamon
1-1/2 c. milk

1 c. cooked sweet potato,
   mashed
1/4 c. butter, melted
1 egg, beaten

Whisk together all ingredients just until dry ingredients are
moistened. Spoon batter into a greased 8" cast-iron skillet or pan.
Bake at 425 degrees for 30 minutes or until a toothpick inserted in
center comes out clean. Makes 6 servings.

If the weather is sunny and blue-skied, take your Thanksgiving
feast outdoors. Set up a table under the leaves, or turn it into
a barn party. Layer woolen blankets on the table, then mix &
match painted chairs for seating. Make dinner fun!

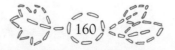

The *Thanksgiving* Table

Praline Yams

Sandy Groezinger
Stockton, IL

I first tasted these yams over 10 years ago at a Thanksgiving gathering...I just had to have the recipe! Now this is my favorite way to prepare yams.

40-oz. can yams, drained
   and cubed
1/2 c. chopped pecans
1/2 c. sweetened flaked coconut

1/2 c. brown sugar, packed
1/4 c. all-purpose flour
1/4 c. butter, melted

Place yams in an ungreased 2-quart casserole dish. Combine remaining ingredients in a small bowl; blend well and sprinkle over yams. Bake, uncovered, at 350 degrees for 35 to 40 minutes, until bubbly. Serves 8 to 10.

Add a little autumn crunch to Praline Yams...sprinkle toasted pumpkin seeds on before popping the casserole dish into the oven.

Thanksgiving Pumpkin Pie

Paula Marchesi
Lenhartsville, PA

I learned at a very early age to always save room for dessert...especially on Thanksgiving day when my mom made homemade pie from scratch. It smelled so good while it was baking, I could hardly wait to have a slice!

1 c. all-purpose flour
1/2 c. walnuts, ground
1/3 c. butter, softened
1/4 c. brown sugar, packed
1/4 t. cinnamon
15-oz. can pumpkin
14-oz. can sweetened
  condensed milk
3-oz. pkg. cream cheese,
  softened

1 egg, beaten
1 t. vanilla extract
1 t. pumpkin pie spice
1/4 t. nutmeg
1/4 t. ground cloves
1/2 t. salt
1/4 c. half-and-half
3/4 c. hot water
Garnish: whipped cream

Combine flour, walnuts, butter, brown sugar and cinnamon. Press firmly into the bottom and up the sides of a lightly greased 10" springform pan. Bake at 350 degrees for 20 minutes. In a large bowl, combine pumpkin, condensed milk, cream cheese, egg, vanilla, spices and salt; beat until smooth. Add half-and-half and mix until blended; stir in hot water. Pour into baked crust. Bake at 350 degrees for 50 to 60 minutes, until set. Cool completely. With a knife, loosen sides of pie. Remove sides from springform pan. Serve each slice with a dollop of whipped cream, if desired. Makes 12 servings.

Top off your pumpkin pie with cinnamon-spice whipped cream. In a chilled mixing bowl, beat 2 cups whipping cream, 1 T. orange liqueur and 1/4 t. cinnamon 'til stiff peaks form.

The *Thanksgiving* Table

Frozen Pumpkin Bars

Beverly Ray
Brandon, FL

*When the frost is on the pumpkin, you'll love
serving up this frosty treat!*

2 c. canned pumpkin
1 c. sugar
1 t. salt
1 t. ground ginger
1 t. cinnamon
1/2 t. nutmeg

1/2 gal. vanilla ice cream,
  softened
36 gingersnaps, divided
Optional: whipped cream,
  pecan halves

Mix together pumpkin, sugar, salt and spices. Fold pumpkin mixture into softened ice cream. Line the bottom of a 13"x9" baking pan with half of gingersnaps. Spread half of ice cream mixture over top. Arrange remaining gingersnaps on top; spread with remaining ice cream mixture. Freeze until firm, or overnight. Garnish with whipped cream and pecan halves, if desired. Let stand at room temperature for 5 to 10 minutes before slicing. Serves 15 to 18.

Practical and pretty napkin rings...twist lengths of bittersweet into a circle, tucking in colorful leaves and mums. They're so creative on a Thanksgiving table!

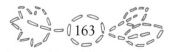

Honey Dutch Apple Pie

Marlene Huffaker
Hagerstown, IN

The basic recipe is my sweet mother-in-law's and it is my husband's favorite. While I've made some slight adjustments, every time I bake it I recall precious memories of my husband's parents.

9-inch pie crust
1/2 c. sugar, divided
3 T. all-purpose flour, divided
1/4 c. honey
1/3 c. fat-free evaporated milk
1/4 t. nutmeg

1/8 t. ground cloves
1-1/2 t. cinnamon, divided
1-1/2 to 2 lbs. tart apples,
   cored, peeled and sliced
1 to 2 T. butter, diced
Garnish: vanilla ice cream

Sprinkle pie crust with one tablespoon each sugar and flour. Combine remaining sugar and flour in a small bowl; stir in honey and evaporated milk. Add nutmeg, cloves and half of cinnamon; mix well. Place apples in a large bowl; pour honey mixture over top. Toss gently to coat; spoon into crust. Sprinkle with remaining cinnamon and dot with butter. Bake at 425 degrees for 35 to 40 minutes, until apples are fork-tender. Reduce heat to 375 degrees. Sprinkle topping over apples; return to oven. Bake for an additional 10 minutes. Serve warm, topped with ice cream. Serves 6 to 8.

Topping:

1/3 c. all-purpose flour
3 T. sugar
3 T. brown sugar, packed

1/8 t. salt
1/4 c. butter

Combine dry ingredients; cut butter into mixture with 2 knives.

The *Thanksgiving* Table

Walnut Raisin Pie

Gloria Kaufmann
Orrville, OH

One of my husband's favorite pies. Have a cup of coffee or tea ready to enjoy with this rich pie.

3 eggs, beaten
2/3 c. sugar
1 c. corn syrup
1/3 c. butter, melted
1/2 t. cinnamon
1/2 t. nutmeg

1/2 t. ground cloves
1/2 t. salt
1 c. walnuts, coarsely chopped
2 c. raisins
9-inch pie crust

In a large bowl, beat together eggs, sugar, corn syrup, butter, spices and salt until well mixed. Stir in walnuts and raisins; pour into pie crust. Bake at 375 degrees for 40 to 50 minutes, until set. Cool before slicing. Serves 6 to 8.

Eggnog Sauce

Linda Cuellar
Riverside, CA

You can serve this sauce warm or cool...either way it's good. Spoon over apple pie, apple dumplings or bread pudding. So yummy!

3 T. all-purpose flour
1/2 t. salt

2 T. sugar
2 c. eggnog

In a double boiler, combine flour, salt and sugar. Stir in eggnog until smooth. Cook over medium heat for 6 to 8 minutes, until thickened. Remove from heat; cool and serve. Makes about 2 cups.

Overnight guests will feel warm & cozy...leave a knitted lap blanket and fluffy bathrobe at the foot of the bed.

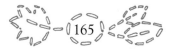

Nutmeg Feather Cake

Faye Mayberry
Saint David, AZ

This recipe was discovered in a vintage cookbook dated 1952. I was instantly intrigued with it because I like nutmeg and have never come upon a strictly nutmeg-flavored cake. We top warm servings with a pat of butter and they are heavenly!

1/4 c. butter, softened
1/4 c. shortening
1-1/2 c. sugar
3 eggs, beaten
2 c. all-purpose flour
1/4 t. salt

1 t. baking powder
1 t. baking soda
2 t. nutmeg
1 c. buttermilk
1/2 t. vanilla extract

Blend together shortening and sugar. Add eggs; beat well. Whisk together flour, salt, baking powder, baking soda and nutmeg; set aside. In a separate small bowl, combine buttermilk and vanilla. Add flour mixture to shortening mixture alternately with buttermilk mixture. Spread in a greased, wax paper-lined 13"x9" baking pan. Bake at 350 degrees for 25 to 30 minutes, or until cake is golden and tests done. Serves 8 to 10.

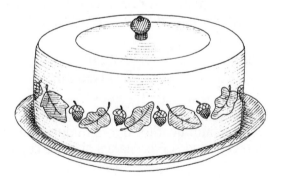

One of the luckiest things that can happen to you in life
is to have a happy childhood.

– Agatha Christie

The *Thanksgiving* Table

Old-Fashioned Butterscotch Pie
Francie Stutzman
Dalton, OH

A favorite for Thanksgiving.

1/2 c. butter	1/2 t. salt
1-1/2 c. brown sugar, packed	2 c. milk
4 c. water	2 egg yolks, beaten
6 T. all-purpose flour	1 t. vanilla extract
1 c. sugar	2 9-inch pie crusts, baked

Combine butter and brown sugar in a large saucepan over medium heat. Cook until lightly golden. Add water; cook for 10 minutes, stirring often. In a medium bowl, mix together flour, sugar and salt. Add milk; stir in yolks. Add to butter mixture, stirring constantly. Cook until thickened, about 10 to 12 minutes. Spread mixture in pie crusts. Refrigerate for 2 to 3 hours. Makes 2 pies; each serves 6 to 8.

Try decorating the Thanksgiving table with white Lumina pumpkins. Hollowed out and filled with bittersweet berries and fall leaves, they bring a fresh, farmhouse look to any room.

Sweet Potato Pie

Cheryl Baker
Springhill, FL

This pie is so good. Every time I give one to someone, they either beg for the recipe or beg me to make another one. The original recipe was from my mother, but I tweaked it over the years into what it is now.

2 c. sweet potatoes, peeled,
    cooked and mashed
2 eggs, beaten
1-1/4 c. sugar
1/4 c. butter, melted
1 c. evaporated milk or
    whipping cream

1 t. cinnamon
1 t. vanilla extract
9-inch pie crust
Garnish: whipped topping

Mix together mashed sweet potatoes, eggs and sugar. Add butter, milk or cream, cinnamon and vanilla; spread in pie crust. Bake at 350 degrees for one hour and 15 minutes; cool. Serve with a dollop of whipped topping. Serves 6 to 8.

Tuck votives inside Mason jars and set in the middle
of urns last used to hold summer's flowers. Surround the jars
with nuts, berries, hedge apples, gourds, mini pumpkins
and leaves...oh-so pretty.

Whipped Pumpkin Pie

Sarina Skidmore
Buffalo, MO

I created this recipe for my son, who is allergic to dairy products. Until trying this recipe, he had never had a pumpkin pie. Now he and the rest of my family ask for Whipped Pumpkin Pie!

15-oz. can pumpkin
2 10-oz. pkgs. mini
    marshmallows
1 t. cinnamon
12-oz. container frozen non-dairy
    whipped topping, thawed

2 9-inch graham cracker crusts
Optional: additional whipped
    topping

Combine pumpkin, marshmallows and cinnamon in a heavy saucepan. Stir over low heat until marshmallows are melted. Remove from heat; cover and let stand until mixture reaches room temperature. Fold in whipped topping. Divide evenly into pie crusts; chill for one hour before serving. If desired, garnish with dollops of whipped topping. Makes 2 pies; each serves 6 to 8.

A treat everyone loves and is so quick to prepare...be sure to keep lots of these in the freezer. Simply place a scoop of softened cinnamon ice cream between 2 oatmeal or ginger cookies. Wrap in wax paper and freeze...yummy!

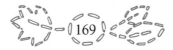

Colorado Pear Pie

Dana Casteele Kohut
Prospect, OH

I discovered this tasty pie on a family trip to Colorado. It was being served in a train depot that had been renovated into a restaurant. We loved the pie so much, I had to make one! After coming home, I pulled out several recipes and combined them into one scrumptious pie our whole family loves.

9-inch pie crust
1 c. plus 1 t. sugar, divided
2 T. cornstarch
1 T. cinnamon

5 c. pears, cored, peeled and
   thinly sliced
2 t. vanilla extract
1 egg white, beaten

On a lightly floured counter, roll out crust to a 16-inch circle, 1/8-inch thick. Transfer to an aluminum foil-lined baking sheet. Press out any creases; set aside. In a large bowl, combine one cup sugar, cornstarch and cinnamon. Add pears and vanilla; toss gently to coat. Spoon pears into center of crust, spreading them to within 2 inches of edge. Fold crust up over pears to form a border of about 2 inches, pleating and folding crust as needed. Brush folded edge with egg white and sprinkle with remaining sugar. Bake at 350 degrees until pears are tender and crust is lightly golden, about 20 minutes. Cool slightly on a wire rack before serving. Serves 6.

Fresh fruit makes such a pretty centerpiece. For a new twist, dip the bottom half of pears in water, then dust with sanding sugar. Piled in a wooden bowl, they're so pretty. To keep them their freshest, put them in the refrigerator and place on the table just before family & friends arrive.

Thanksgiving
on a
Bun

What to do the day after Thanksgiving...

Watch your favorite classic movies,

put a big pot of turkey soup on the stove,

get a start on holiday cards,

decorate for Christmas,

dare to go shopping or...

stay in your jammies all day, enjoy a cup of orange-clove tea and RELAX!

Thanksgiving on a *Bun*

Overnight Scalloped Turkey

Pat Habiger
Spearville, KS

A make-ahead meal that just can't be beat.

2 10-3/4 oz. cans cream of
  mushroom soup
2-1/2 c. milk
8-oz. pkg. pasteurized process
  cheese spread, cubed
4 c. cooked turkey, chopped

7-oz. pkg. elbow macaroni,
  uncooked
3 eggs, hard-boiled, peeled
  and chopped
1/2 c. butter, melted and divided
1-1/2 c. soft bread crumbs

In a large bowl, combine soup, milk and cheese; add turkey, macaroni and eggs. Stir in 1/4 cup melted butter; transfer to a greased 13"x9" baking pan. Cover and refrigerate for 8 hours or overnight. Toss bread crumbs with remaining butter; sprinkle over top. Bake, uncovered, at 350 degrees for 55 to 60 minutes, until bubbly and golden. Serves 8 to 10.

The day after Thanksgiving is a great day for families to enjoy being together. How about a pumpkin relay race? Racers line up, each with a pumpkin, and use a stick to roll the pumpkins to the finish line. Little ones may want to use their hands instead of a stick...memory-making fun!

Aztec Turkey

Fawn McKenzie
Wenatchee, WA

A wonderful recipe for turkey leftovers. Growing up, I remember it being so comforting on those cold Montana nights.

10-3/4 oz. can cream of chicken soup
10-3/4 oz. can cream of mushroom soup
1 c. milk
1/4 c. sweet onion, chopped
1 doz. 6-inch corn tortillas, sliced into strips

2 to 2-1/2 c. cooked turkey, chopped
2 4-oz. cans whole green chiles, sliced lengthwise and seeds removed
8-oz. pkg. shredded Cheddar cheese

Mix soups with milk and onion. In a lightly greased 13"x9" baking pan, layer half each tortilla strips, turkey, soup mixture and chiles. Repeat layers, ending with chiles. Sprinkle with shredded cheese. Bake, uncovered, at 350 degrees for one hour. Serves 6 to 8.

Gobbler Bake

Connie Bryant
Topeka, KS

When kids are little, they say such funny things. Out daughter Molly named this dish when she was 5, and it's been that ever since.

3 c. prepared stuffing
2-3/4 oz. can French fried onions, divided
10-3/4 oz. can cream of celery soup

3/4 c. milk
1-1/2 c. cooked turkey, cubed
10-oz. pkg. frozen green peas, thawed

Combine stuffing and half of onions. Spoon mixture into a lightly greased 9"x9" baking pan, pressing it into bottom and up sides of pan. Blend remaining ingredients; pour over stuffing. Bake, covered, at 350 degrees for 30 minutes. Uncover; top with remaining onions. Bake for an additional 5 minutes. Serves 4 to 6.

Thanksgiving on a *Bun*

Fiesta Enchiladas

Nancy Ramsey
Delaware, OH

*A college roommate made this recipe after we'd grown tired of
endless turkey sandwiches...what a hit!*

8-oz. pkg. shredded Cheddar
  cheese
1 onion, chopped
2-oz. can sliced black olives,
  drained

1 T. oil
24 6-inch corn tortillas
19-oz. can enchilada sauce
4 c. cooked turkey, chopped

Combine cheese, onion and olives in a small bowl; set aside. Heat oil
in a skillet over medium heat; add tortillas a few at a time and cook
until soft. Dip tortillas in sauce to coat. Spoon turkey and cheese
mixture into center of each tortilla; roll up and place 12 enchiladas
in a lightly greased 13"x9" baking pan. Spread enough of remaining
sauce to cover. Make a second layer of enchiladas; spread remaining
sauce on top and sprinkle with remaining cheese mixture. Bake at
350 degrees for 20 minutes, or until cheese is melted. Serves 6.

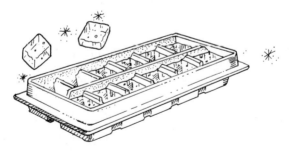

Sauté onions, celery and carrots left from the appetizer tray
in a bit of oil until tender, divide among ice cube trays,
then cover with broth. Freeze; then store cubes in a plastic
zipping bag and keep frozen...they'll add instant flavor
to soups, sauces and stews.

Tangy Turkey Salad Croissants

Wendy Jacobs
Idaho Falls, ID

*The day after Thanksgiving, my mom, sisters and I decided we wanted
more than just the "usual" turkey sandwich. We combined some
of our favorite flavors and came up with these...we love 'em!*

2 c. cooked turkey breast, cubed
1/2 c. cranberries, finely
  chopped
1 orange, peeled and chopped
1/2 c. mayonnaise
1 t. mustard

1 t. sugar
1/2 t. salt
1/4 c. chopped pecans
6 croissants, split
Garnish: lettuce leaves

In a large bowl, combine turkey, cranberries, orange, mayonnaise,
mustard, sugar and salt; chill. Just before serving, stir in pecans.
Top each croissant with 1/2 cup turkey mixture and a lettuce leaf.
Makes 6 sandwiches.

California Turkey Club

Melanie Lowe
Dover, DE

*Our family went to Oakland, California last month to attend our
nephew's wedding reception. These were served at a family
luncheon the next day...scrumptious!*

1/2 c. mayonnaise
1/4 c. salsa
8 slices country-style bread
4 lettuce leaves
8 slices tomato

8 slices cooked turkey
8 slices bacon, crisply cooked
8 slices Cheddar cheese
2 avocados, pitted, peeled
  and sliced

Combine mayonnaise and salsa; spread onto 4 slices of bread. Layer
with lettuce, tomato, turkey, bacon, cheese and avocado. Top with
remaining bread. Makes 4 sandwiches.

Thanksgiving on a *Bun*

Apricot-Cashew Salad

Rhonda Reeder
Ellicott City, MD

*So versatile...the kids enjoy this for lunch as a wrap, but I've
also served it over red leaf lettuce for a ladies' luncheon at church.*

2 c. cooked turkey, diced
1 Granny Smith apple, cored,
   peeled and diced
1 c. celery, chopped
1/4 c. dried apricots, finely
   chopped
1/2 c. cashews, chopped

1/2 c. mayonnaise
1/4 c. sour cream
2 T. apricot preserves
1/4 t. ground ginger
1/8 t. nutmeg
1/8 t. pepper

In a large bowl, toss together turkey, apple, celery, apricots and
cashews; set aside. Whisk together remaining ingredients; spoon
over turkey mixture and fold in until well blended. Serves 4.

Keep a container in your freezer for leftover vegetables.
When you are ready to make soup or stew,
just add them...so handy!

Stuffed Shells

Brittney Golden
Aliquippa, PA

This recipe can be made up to 3 days ahead...just assemble, refrigerate and then add a few minutes to the cooking time.

4 c. cooked turkey or
   chicken, diced
3 cloves garlic, minced
2 6-oz. pkgs. chicken-flavored
   stuffing mix, prepared

12-oz. pkg. jumbo shell
   pasta, cooked
2 10-3/4 oz. cans cream of
   chicken soup
1-1/4 c. milk

In a lightly greased skillet over medium heat, sauté turkey or chicken and garlic for about 10 minutes. Add stuffing; mix well. Spoon mixture into shells. Arrange shells seam-side up in a lightly greased 11"x7" baking pan; set aside. Combine soup and milk; spoon 3/4 of soup mixture over shells. Refrigerate remaining soup mixture. Bake, covered, at 350 degrees for about one hour. Serves 6 to 8.

Spend the day catching up on scrapbooking. Girlfriends, grandmas, aunts and moms will enjoy creating a favorite recipe book. It's easy to include everyone's favorites by making color copies of recipe cards in their handwriting.

Thanksgiving on a *Bun*

Cheddar Ham Pie

Edward Smulski
Lyons, IL

If you have leftover ham, this pie is a guaranteed dinnertime success...everyone will want seconds.

1-1/2 c. cooked ham, cubed
1/2 c. shredded Cheddar cheese
1/3 c. green onion, chopped
1/2 c. biscuit baking mix
1 c. milk

1/3 c. mayonnaise
2 eggs, beaten
1/4 t. pepper
1 T. Dijon mustard
1 T. fresh parsley, chopped

Sprinkle ham, cheese and onion into a lightly greased 9" pie plate. Whisk together remaining ingredients until well blended; pour into pie plate. Bake at 400 degrees for 30 to 40 minutes, until a knife inserted in center comes out clean. Let stand for 5 minutes before serving. Serves 4 to 6.

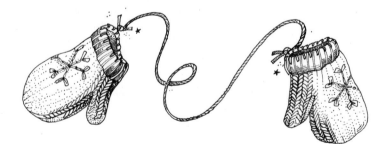

Bundle everyone up in their merriest mittens, hats and coats and go outdoors! While everyone's home, it's the perfect time to take photos for this year's Christmas cards.

Easy Tortilla Soup

Jennifer Halvorson
Richardton, ND

My family requests this easy soup for supper more often than anything else I make. And it is so easy, I can whip it up in no time, even on the busiest night. For a twist, use Cheddar cheese soup with one cup of your favorite salsa.

3 to 4 c. cooked turkey, cubed
2 10-3/4 oz. cans cream of
   chicken soup
2 10-3/4 oz. cans nacho
   cheese soup

15-oz. can enchilada sauce
2-1/2 c. milk
Garnish: shredded Cheddar
   cheese, crushed tortilla chips,
   salsa, sour cream

In a Dutch oven over medium heat, combine all ingredients except garnish. Cook and stir until heated through. Garnish as desired. Makes 6 to 8 servings.

With leftovers on the menu, dinner will be a breeze,
so settle in for some good old-fashioned storytelling.
Tell childhood stories, share funny memories and
exciting adventures...enjoy the memories.

Thanksgiving on a *Bun*

Lemony Sage Mayonnaise

Stacie Avner
Delaware, OH

Top sandwiches with this spread...it's packed with flavor!

2 c. mayonnaise
1/2 c. fresh sage, finely chopped,
   or 3 T. dried sage
2 T. lemon juice

1 T. plus 1 t. lemon zest
1 T. garlic, minced
1 t. pepper

Whisk together all ingredients; cover and refrigerate. Makes about 2 cups.

Sam's Terrific Tortillas

Athena Colegrove
Big Springs, TX

*The fresh flavor combination makes these tortillas outstanding.
Our whole family agrees...my brother Sam had a hit on his hands
when he "tossed" these together.*

10 10-inch flour tortillas
10 slices cooked turkey, sliced
   into thin strips
1 avocado, pitted, peeled
   and sliced

1/2 c. sour cream
1/2 c. shredded Cheddar cheese

Heat flour tortillas in a large skillet over medium heat until slightly browned. Divide turkey strips, avocado, sour cream and cheese among the warmed tortillas. Fold in half and serve. Makes 10 servings.

Old-Fashioned Turkey Pot Pie

Kelly Alderson
Erie, PA

Going to Grandma's for the holidays is like stepping back in time...
a crackling fire in the fireplace, a teakettle singing on the stove
and family gathered 'round the table.

2 9-inch pie crusts
2 T. onion, chopped
1 to 2 t. oil
2 c. frozen mixed vegetables,
   thawed

2 c. cooked turkey, cubed
10-3/4 oz. can cream of
   chicken soup
1/2 c. milk

Line a 9" pie plate with one crust; set aside. In a skillet over medium heat, sauté onion in oil until slightly soft. Mix together vegetables, turkey, onion, soup and milk; pour into pie crust. Cover with remaining crust; crimp edges and cut vents in crust. Bake at 400 degrees for 40 to 50 minutes. Serves 6.

Caroline's Turkey & Dumplings

Elizabeth Blackstone
Racine, WI

A farmer's wife, Caroline's recipes are hearty and filling...
they have to be, come harvest time!

3 c. cooked turkey, chopped
4 c. chicken broth
2 10-3/4 oz. cans cream
   of chicken soup

2 t. chicken bouillon granules
1 t. seasoned pepper
7-1/2 oz. tube refrigerated
   buttermilk biscuits

In a large pot, bring all ingredients except biscuits to a boil. Separate each biscuit in half, making 2 rounds per biscuit. Cut rounds in half. Drop biscuits, one at a time, into boiling broth; stir. Cover; reduce heat to low. Simmer, stirring occasionally, for 15 to 20 minutes. Makes 6 servings.

Thanksgiving on a *Bun*

Mom's Day-After Casserole

Geneva Rogers
Gillette, WY

When our family gathers at Thanksgiving, it means wagon rides, football games and crafts with the kids. Mom outdoes herself in the kitchen, and this casserole creation of hers is an all-time favorite.

5 T. butter, divided
2 T. all-purpose flour
12-oz. can evaporated milk
1 c. water
1/4 t. onion powder
1/4 t. salt

1/4 t. pepper
1 c. herb-flavored stuffing mix, finely crushed
1 c. cooked turkey, diced
1 c. shredded Cheddar cheese
2 c. mashed potatoes

Melt 3 tablespoons butter in a saucepan over low heat; blend in flour. Slowly stir in evaporated milk and water; sprinkle with seasonings. Cook and stir over low heat for 5 minutes; set aside. Melt remaining butter; toss with stuffing mix and set aside. Place turkey in a lightly greased 13"x9" baking pan. Pour milk mixture over turkey; sprinkle with cheese. Spread mashed potatoes over cheese; spoon stuffing mixture over top. Bake at 350 degrees for 45 minutes, until hot and bubbly. Serves 8.

One of the best ways to give thanks is to help someone else. Volunteer, lend a neighbor a hand, leave a surprise on someone's doorstep...thoughtful ways to show you care.

Swiss-Ham Noodle Casserole

Anne Marie Wherthey
Rice Lake, WI

A family favorite that's so easy to make.

2 T. margarine
1/2 c. onion, chopped
1/2 c. green pepper, chopped
10-3/4 oz. can cream of
    mushroom soup
8-oz. container sour cream

8-oz. pkg. rotini pasta, cooked
    and drained
8-oz. pkg. shredded Swiss
    cheese
2 c. cooked ham, cubed

Melt margarine in a skillet over medium heat. Add onion and pepper; cook until tender. Stir in soup and sour cream. In a lightly greased 3-quart casserole dish, layer half each of the noodles, cheese, ham and soup mixture; repeat layering. Bake, uncovered, at 350 degrees for 45 to 50 minutes, until heated through. Serves 6.

The most remarkable thing about my mother is that for thirty years she served the family nothing but leftovers. The original meal has never been found.

– Calvin Trillin

Thanksgiving on a *Bun*

Oh-So Cheesy Tetrazzini

Vickie
Gooseberry Patch

Filled to the brim with cheese and savory flavors.

3 T. butter
1 c. sliced mushrooms
1 onion, chopped
1 red pepper, chopped
1 clove garlic, chopped
1/4 c. all-purpose flour
2 c. chicken broth
1 c. whipping cream
1 c. milk

1/2 c. shredded Swiss cheese
1/2 c. shredded Cheddar cheese
1/2 c. grated Parmesan cheese
1/2 t. dried thyme
1/2 t. salt
1/4 t. pepper
2 c. cooked turkey, diced
16-oz. pkg. spaghetti, cooked

In a large skillet, melt butter over medium heat. Add mushrooms, onion, red pepper and garlic; sauté for 5 minutes. Sprinkle with flour; cook and stir for one minute. Slowly stir in broth, cream and milk; simmer for one minute, until thickened. Remove from heat. Add cheeses and stir until melted; mix in seasonings and turkey. Toss with cooked spaghetti and spread into a lightly greased 13"x9" baking pan. Bake, uncovered, at 350 degrees for 25 to 30 minutes, until bubbly. Let stand for 10 minutes before serving. Serves 8.

Call up your best girlfriends and enjoy shopping the day after Thanksgiving. Meet very early... have some scrumptious breakfast goodies to fortify yourselves, then go! Afterward, invite everyone back for a leisurely lunch and talk about all the fabulous bargains you found.

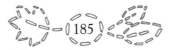

Stuffed Crescent Rolls

Sharon Tillman
Hampton, VA

When a family reunion found us traveling to Wyoming, we stopped along the way at a roadside diner. I ordered the tastiest turkey-filled crescent rolls, and when we returned home, I was determined to duplicate the recipe. My family says these are just as good, and they couldn't be simpler to whip up.

1 t. butter
1/2 c. celery, finely chopped
1/4 c. onion, finely chopped
2 c. cooked turkey, finely
   chopped

10-3/4 oz. can cream of
   mushroom soup
3 8-oz. tubes refrigerated
   crescent rolls
dill weed to taste

Melt butter in a skillet over medium heat. Add celery and onion; cook for 3 to 4 minutes, until tender. Add turkey and soup; mix well. Remove from heat. Separate crescent rolls into 24 triangles. Place one tablespoon turkey mixture on wide end of each triangle; roll up from wide end. Place rolls seam-side down on greased baking sheets, 2 inches apart. Curve ends to form crescent shape. Sprinkle with dill weed. Bake at 350 degrees for 8 to 9 minutes, until golden. Serve immediately. Makes 2 dozen.

Put a casserole in the slow-cooker and spend the day decorating. This year, why not use some of your holiday decorations in an unexpected way? Place some of your favorite ornaments in a glass hurricane, put your nativity set on a kitchen windowsill or hang a Christmas wreath on the staircase.

Thanksgiving on a *Bun*

Southwest Turkey Salad

Kendall Hale
Lynn, MA

If you love the flavor, but not the heat, try planting the "Fooled You" variety of jalapeños...all the taste, but none of the heat!

5 c. cooked turkey, chopped
1 c. celery, finely chopped
1 jalapeño pepper, seeded
   and diced
3 T. sweet pickle relish

1 c. mayonnaise
1 T. dried cilantro
2 t. salt
2 t. pepper

In a large bowl, combine turkey, celery, jalapeño, relish and mayonnaise. Sprinkle with cilantro, salt and pepper. Mix well; refrigerate until ready to serve. Serves 4 to 6.

Sun-Dried Tomato Mayonnaise

Jill Webb
Christiansburg, VA

I love the fancy herbed mayonnaise sometimes served on sandwiches at cafes. I also love sun-dried tomatoes, so one day I decided to try to combine the flavors and make my own. I think it's perfect!

1/2 c. mayonnaise
1 t. garlic, minced
1-1/2 t. dried parsley

1/8 t. dried thyme
2 to 4 slices sun-dried tomatoes
salt and pepper to taste

Combine all ingredients in a food processor; process to desired consistency. Refrigerate 2 hours before serving. Makes about 1/2 cup.

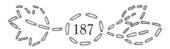

Grandma's Dinner Dish

Joan Wright
Marquette, MI

This is my grandmother's recipe, and is still requested by my grown children when they visit. Make it to suit your taste...in place of corn, try green beans or undiluted cream of celery soup.

1 lb. ground beef
1 onion, diced
salt and pepper to taste

14-3/4 oz. can creamed corn
2 c. mashed potatoes
1/4 c. butter, diced

Brown ground beef and onion in a skillet over medium heat; drain. Sprinkle with salt and pepper. Spread beef mixture in a lightly greased one-quart casserole dish; spoon creamed corn over beef. Top with mashed potatoes; dot with butter. Bake, uncovered, at 350 degrees for 45 minutes. Turn oven to broil; broil until potatoes are golden. Serves 4.

Host your own chef competition! It's fun to see who can turn yesterday's juicy turkey or savory stuffing into an exciting new recipe...you may just create a brand-new family favorite.

Thanksgiving on a *Bun*

Swiss Noodle Bake

Jill Valentine
Jackson, TN

I admit it...my friends and I get up at daybreak the Friday after Thanksgiving to go shopping! Several hours later, absolutely exhausted, we come back to my home for lunch. With leftover turkey on hand, this recipe is a snap to make and bakes in less than 30 minutes.

2 c. wide egg noodles, cooked
10-oz. pkg. frozen chopped
  broccoli, cooked and drained
2 T. butter
2 T. all-purpose flour
1/2 t. dry mustard

1 t. salt
1/4 t. pepper
1-1/2 c. milk
1 c. shredded Swiss cheese
2 c. cooked turkey, cubed
1/2 c. slivered almonds, toasted

Combine noodles and broccoli in a large bowl; set aside. In a large saucepan, melt butter over medium heat. Stir in flour, mustard, salt and pepper until smooth. Gradually add milk; bring to a boil. Cook and stir for 2 minutes, or until thickened. Remove from heat; stir in cheese until melted. Add turkey; pour over noodle mixture and toss to mix. Transfer to a greased 1-1/2 quart casserole dish; sprinkle with almonds. Bake, uncovered, at 350 degrees for 20 to 25 minutes, until heated through. Serves 4.

Whip up a tasty sandwich spread in no time. Simply combine leftover turkey or ham in a food processor with a little mayonnaise. Make it more flavorful by adding seasonings, chopped vegetables or pickles.

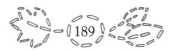

Ham & Potato Casserole

Kathy Grashoff
Fort Wayne, IN

This dish has a rich, cheesy flavor.

2-1/2 c. cooked ham, diced
26-oz. pkg. frozen shredded
  potatoes
10-3/4 oz. can cream of potato
  soup

1/2 t. pepper
1/4 c. grated Parmesan cheese
1 c. sharp Cheddar cheese,
  shredded
Optional: paprika to taste

Combine ham, potatoes, soup and pepper. Spoon mixture into a lightly greased 13"x9" baking pan. Bake, uncovered, at 400 degrees for 25 minutes. Sprinkle with cheeses and paprika, if using. Bake for an additional 5 minutes, or until heated through and cheese melts. Serves 4 to 6.

A little gravy added to diced turkey and vegetables is
a quick & easy filling for pot pie. Spooned into a pie crust,
or placed in a casserole dish and topped with a layer
of biscuits or mashed potatoes, it can be heated
in the oven in no time...comfort food, fast.

Thanksgiving on a *Bun*

Ritzy Turkey Casserole

Wanda Wilson
Hamilton, GA

*During the busy holiday season, this casserole is a quick fix,
and nice enough for company.*

16-oz. can French-style green
   beans, drained
15-oz. can shoepeg corn,
   drained
1/2 c. celery, chopped
Optional: 1/2 c. green pepper,
   chopped
1/2 c. onion, chopped
1/2 c. sour cream

10-3/4 oz. can cream of celery
   soup
salt and pepper to taste
1/2 c. slivered almonds
2 c. cooked turkey or chicken,
   cubed
12-oz. pkg. round buttery
   crackers, divided
1/2 c. butter, melted

Mix together all ingredients except crackers and butter in a large
bowl; spread in a lightly greased 13"x9" baking pan. Crush half the
crackers; reserve remaining crackers for another recipe. Combine
crushed crackers with melted butter; sprinkle over casserole. Bake
at 350 degrees for 45 minutes. Makes 6 servings.

There are so many ways to serve mashed potatoes...turn them
into crispy potato pancakes, spoon over any casserole for a quick
Shepherd's Pie or scoop into a bowl and top with gravy, chopped
turkey and corn for a homestyle dinner-in-a-bowl.

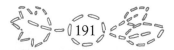

Rhonda's White Chili

Rhonda Hauenstein
Tell City, IN

This is a favorite of my family's, and a perfect recipe for leftover Thanksgiving or Christmas turkey. I like to serve it alongside homemade bread or biscuits.

1 onion, chopped
Optional: 1 banana pepper,
   seeded and chopped
2 cloves garlic, minced
4 c. chicken broth
2 16-oz. cans black-eyed peas,
   drained and rinsed

2 T. fresh parsley, minced
1 T. lime juice
1 to 1-1/4 t. ground cumin
2 T. cornstarch
1/4 c. cold water
3 to 4 c. cooked turkey, chopped

In a large kettle over medium heat, combine onion, garlic, banana pepper, if using, broth, black-eyed peas, parsley, lime juice and cumin; bring to a boil. Reduce heat; cover and simmer for 10 minutes, stirring occasionally. Mix together cornstarch and water until smooth; stir into chili. Add turkey. Bring to a boil; cook and stir for 2 minutes, or until thickened. Makes 6 servings.

Bread not used in Grandma's stuffing easily becomes the best homemade croutons for soups and salads. Blend favorite herbs and spices with 1/4 cup olive oil and brush on both sides of bread slices; cut into cubes. Place in a single layer on a baking sheet and bake in a 300-degree oven until crisp, about 45 minutes. Let cool and store in an airtight container, then use within one week.

Thanksgiving on a *Bun*

Sweet Potato Cranberry Muffins

Jackie Smulski
Lyons, IL

You'll love the these deliciously different cranberry muffins!

1-1/2 c. all-purpose flour	1 egg, beaten
1/2 c. sugar	1/2 c. milk
2 t. baking powder	1/2 c. mashed sweet potatoes
3/4 t. salt	1/4 c. butter, melted
1/2 t. cinnamon	1 c. cranberries, chopped
1/2 t. nutmeg	cinnamon-sugar to taste

Combine flour, sugar, baking powder, salt and spices in a large bowl; set aside. In a separate bowl, combine egg, milk, sweet potatoes and butter; stir into flour mixture just until moistened. Fold in cranberries. Fill paper-lined muffin cups 1/2 full; sprinkle with cinnamon-sugar. Bake at 375 degrees for 20 to 22 minutes, until a toothpick tests clean. Cool completely. Makes one dozen.

Don't just think dinner, use leftovers to make savory breakfast omelets. Fill omelets with chopped turkey, sautéed vegetables and shredded cheese...delicious!

Very Berry Bread

Jo Ann
Gooseberry Patch

*Cranberry sauce is the secret ingredient in this moist,
tangy quick bread.*

2-1/2 c. sugar
1 c. shortening
3 eggs, beaten
3 ripe bananas, mashed
1 c. cranberry sauce
1/2 c. milk
1 t. vanilla extract

4 c. all-purpose flour
1-1/2 t. baking powder
1-1/2 t. baking soda
1 t. cinnamon
1/2 t. nutmeg
1/2 c. chopped walnuts

In a large bowl, blend together sugar and shortening until light and fluffy. Beat in eggs; stir in bananas, cranberry sauce, milk and vanilla. In a separate bowl, mix together flour, baking soda, baking powder and spices. Gradually blend flour mixture into banana mixture; fold in walnuts. Pour into 2 greased 9"x5" loaf pans. Bake at 350 degrees for 50 to 60 minutes, until a toothpick inserted in center comes out clean. Cool in pans for 10 minutes; turn out onto a wire rack and cool completely. Makes 2 loaves.

Turn leftover fruit into a sweet & simple dessert. Just add fruit to a blender and purée, then layer in dessert glasses over cubes of pound cake and top with whipped cream. Oh-so easy!

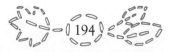

Thanksgiving on a *Bun*

Grandma's Fruitcake Cookies

Luanne McDuffie
Rockingham, NC

My grandmother would make these each year right after Thanksgiving and allow the grandchildren to have "just one" if we were well-behaved. It was such a thrill when she would open the large tin she kept them in, fold back the cloth cover and reach inside to get one.

1/2 c. shortening
1 c. brown sugar, packed
1 egg, beaten
1/4 c. buttermilk
1-3/4 c. all-purpose flour
1/4 t. baking soda

1/2 t. salt
1/2 c. chopped pecans
1 c. chopped dates
1 c. candied cherries, chopped
Garnish: pecan halves, candied
    cherries

Mix together shortening, brown sugar and egg in a large bowl; stir in buttermilk. Combine flour, baking soda and salt; add to shortening mixture. Stir in pecans, dates and cherries; chill in refrigerator for at least 30 minutes. Drop by teaspoonfuls 2 inches apart on greased baking sheets. Top each cookie with a pecan half or candied cherry. Bake at 400 degrees for 8 to 10 minutes. Makes 4 dozen.

Bake & take! Everyone loves cookies, so make the day after Thanksgiving a day to bake up your favorites. Once all the baking and sampling is done, send family & friends home with batches of cookies to enjoy on their way.

Frosty Cranberry Parfaits

Regina Wickline
Pebble Beach, CA

Dress up dessert with this 2-ingredient recipe...so scrumptious!

8-oz. container frozen whipped topping, thawed

1 c. cranberry sauce

Combine topping and cranberry sauce; mix well. Freeze until partially frozen. Serve in parfait cups. Makes 4 servings.

Serve parfaits in vintage juice glasses...the colors
are so cheery and bright!

Gifts that say
Thanks!

Gift tags to copy, cut & color!

from the kitchen of:

to:

from:

Make a copy of these little tags & tie them on gifts from your kitchen to make them extra special.

Gifts that say *Thanks!*

Maine Maple Candies

Jennifer Martineau
Delaware, OH

*These arrived as a Christmas surprise from my granny
in Maine...what a yummy treat!*

14-oz. can sweetened
  condensed milk
1/4 c. butter, softened
2 T. maple flavoring

1-1/2 c. chopped nuts
32-oz. pkg. powdered sugar
3 8-oz. pkgs. semi-sweet
  chocolate, chopped

Mix together condensed milk, butter, flavoring and nuts; gradually
beat in powdered sugar. Roll into one-inch balls. Refrigerate until
ready to dip. Melt chocolate in a heavy saucepan over low heat; dip
balls into chocolate. Place on wax paper-lined baking sheets until set.
Keep refrigerated. Makes 3 dozen.

Babchi's Maple Fudge

Paula Marchesi
Lenhartsville, PA

*My grandkids call me Babchi, the Polish word for grandma, and each
year they enjoy this wonderful autumn treat...the same sweet treat
that I made for my own children when they were growing up.*

1-1/2 c. sugar
2/3 c. evaporated milk
2 T. butter
1/4 t. salt
2 c. mini marshmallows

2 c. white chocolate chips
1/2 c. chopped walnuts
1-1/2 t. maple flavoring
48 walnut halves

Combine sugar, evaporated milk, butter and salt in a large, heavy
saucepan. Bring to a rolling boil over medium heat, stirring constantly
for 4-1/2 to 5 minutes. Remove from heat. Stir in marshmallows,
chocolate chips, walnuts and flavoring. Stir vigorously for one minute,
or until marshmallows and chocolate are melted. Pour into an aluminum
foil-lined 13"x9" baking pan. Press walnut halves into fudge in rows,
spacing each 1/2-inch apart. Chill until firm, about one hour. Cut into
squares to serve. Makes 4 dozen.

Sharon's Apple Jam

Sharon Fruth
Williamsville, NY

My girlfriend and I have made several batches of this scrumptious jam this year for gifts...great on pancakes, waffles, ice cream or toast.

6 c. Granny Smith apples,
    peeled, cored and diced
1/2 c. water
1/2 t. butter
1-3/4 oz. pkg. powdered
    fruit pectin

3 c. sugar
2 c. brown sugar, packed
1/2 t. cinnamon
1/4 t. nutmeg
6 1/2-pint canning jars and
    lids, sterilized

Combine apples, water and butter in a large saucepan. Cook and stir over low heat until apples are soft. Stirring constantly, add pectin and bring to a full boil. Add sugars and spices. Return to a rolling boil, stirring for just one minute. Remove from heat. Pour into hot sterilized jars, leaving 1/4-inch headspace. Wipe rims; secure with lids and rings. Process in a boiling water bath for 10 minutes; set jars on a towel to cool. Check for seals. Makes 6 jars.

Use mini clothespins to attach gift tags and instructions when giving gifts from the kitchen...so clever!

Gifts that say *Thanks!*

Gourmet Apples

Sheri Dulaney
Englewood, OH

Not only do these make a wonderful dessert, they also make delicious gifts! If you're not giving these apples right away, store them in the refrigerator. Just pull out for a few hours before eating to soften the caramel.

4 to 6 Red Delicious apples
4 to 6 wooden skewers
14-oz. pkg. caramels,
  unwrapped
12-oz. pkg. milk chocolate chips

Garnish: crushed chocolate sandwich cookies, multi-colored sprinkles, crushed pecans or walnuts

Wash and dry apples; insert sticks into stem end of apples and set aside. Melt caramel candies in a double boiler over medium heat; remove from heat. Place chocolate chips in a microwave-safe dish; microwave on high setting, stirring every 15 seconds, until melted. Dip apples into melted caramel, then into melted chocolate. Immediately roll apples in desired garnish. Set apples on buttered wax paper; cool completely. Place apples in cellophane bags; tie bags with fabric or ribbon. Makes 4 to 6.

Gather up all your rubber stamps, stickers and glitter for making the best one-of-a-kind gift tags.

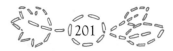

Peanut Butter Popcorn

Jenny Custis
Lynden, WA

The secretary of my elementary school used to make peanut butter popcorn for the teachers to enjoy on their breaks between classes...I can still remember the aroma. I would frequently visit the teachers' lounge to enjoy a bite of this delicious treat. Now I'm a secretary myself and make it for my fellow co-workers and family...it's always a hit and still reminds me of fall.

1/2 c. honey
1/2 c. sugar
1/2 t. vanilla extract
1/2 c. creamy peanut butter
2 qts. popped popcorn

Garnish: seasonal candy-coated chocolates, or any chopped candy for fun, texture and color

Combine honey and sugar over medium heat; bring to a rolling boil. Remove from heat; add vanilla and peanut butter. Drizzle over popped popcorn; toss to mix. Stir in chocolates or candy. Pour onto wax paper and cool completely. Makes about 2 quarts.

Maple Popcorn

Kathryn Hostetler
West Farmington, OH

This popcorn is for sharing...so yummy!

1 c. maple syrup
3 T. butter

1 T. vanilla extract
2 qts. popped popcorn

Combine syrup and butter in a saucepan over medium heat. Cook and stir until mixture reaches the soft-crack stage, or 270 to 289 degrees on a candy thermometer. Remove from heat; add vanilla. Pour over popped popcorn; mix well. Pour onto wax paper and cool completely. Makes about 2 quarts.

Gifts that say *Thanks!*

Holiday Spiced Nuts

Ashley Printz
Ephrata, PA

These nuts are a wonderful snack to make for gift giving over the holidays...I make them every year!

1 egg white
1 t. water
8-oz. jar dry-roasted peanuts
1/2 c. whole almonds

1/2 c. pecan or walnut halves
3/4 c. sugar
1 T. pumpkin pie spice
3/4 t. salt

Beat together egg white and water in a large bowl. Add nuts; stir to coat. Combine remaining ingredients in a separate bowl. Mix well; add to nut mixture, tossing until well coated. Stir until moistened. Spread nut mixture onto a lightly greased 15"x10" jelly-roll pan. Bake at 300 degrees for 25 minutes. Immediately remove nuts onto lightly greased wax paper, spreading into a single layer to dry. Cool completely; break into small pieces. Makes about 4 cups.

Black Walnut Caramels

Denise Nyland
Panama City, FL

Deliver a tin of caramels tucked inside a harvest gathering basket lined with colorful fall leaves.

1 c. sugar
14-oz. can sweetened
   condensed milk
1/4 c. salted butter

1 t. vanilla extract
3/4 c. black walnuts, coarsely
   chopped and lightly toasted

Combine sugar, condensed milk and butter in a heavy saucepan. Stirring constantly, cook over medium heat to firm-ball stage, or 244 to 249 degrees on a candy thermometer. Stir in vanilla and walnuts. Pour into a buttered 9"x9" baking pan. Cool to room temperature. Cut into squares; wrap pieces in plastic wrap or wax paper. Makes 6-1/2 to 7 dozen.

Autumn Moose Mix

Jary Nan Riolo
Bend, OR

I collect moose so when I revamped this mix recipe that I got from a dear friend, I couldn't resist calling it Moose Mix! I can make it for any season by changing the colors of the candies. We enjoy Merry Moose Mix on Christmas, Cupid's Crunch Moose Mix for Valentine's Day and Happy Moose Mix for Easter. Put some in a cute container for a quick gift...it won't last long!

14-oz. pkg. candy-coated chocolates in pumpkin mix colors
14-oz. pkg. candy-coated chocolate peanuts in pumpkin mix colors
16-oz. pkg. candy-coated peanut butter candies
2 11-oz. pkg. candy corn
16-oz. pkgs. bite-size crispy corn bran cereal squares
3 to 4 c. vanilla yogurt-covered raisins
2 12-oz. cans cocktail peanuts

Combine all ingredients in a large bowl. Toss to mix; store in an airtight container. Makes 20 cups.

Hot & Spicy Mixed Nuts

Michelle Rooney
Delaware, OH

What a super teacher gift...spoon these mixed nuts into an apple-shaped tin!

2 c. mixed nuts
3 T. butter
1/8 t. garlic powder
1/8 t. coriander
1/8 t. ground cumin
1/8 t. cayenne pepper
1/4 t. salt

Spread nuts onto an ungreased baking sheet; bake at 350 degrees for 7 minutes. Combine remaining ingredients; mix well. Pour over nuts; toss to mix. Bake for an additional 5 minutes. Makes 2 cups.

Gifts that say *Thanks!*

Cougar Crunch Mix

Marian Buckley
Fontana, CA

When I was a freshman at BYU, this was one of our favorite dorm snacks to munch on while studying for final exams. Now, I make it whenever our family wants a savory treat...ideal for family night.

1-oz. pkg. ranch salad
    dressing mix
2 T. dill weed
6 c. assorted bite-size cereal
    squares

10-oz. pkg. oyster crackers
6-oz. pkg. pretzel sticks, broken
1 c. bagel chips, broken
1/2 c. oil
1/4 c. butter, melted

Mix together dressing mix and dill weed in a large bowl. Add cereal, crackers, pretzels and bagel chips; mix well. Combine oil and butter; drizzle over cereal mixture, tossing to coat well. Place mixture in a large paper bag; let stand for about 2 hours, gently shaking from time to time. Store in an airtight container. Makes 17 to 18 cups.

Gift giving that's so easy...cut the top of a brown paper bag
with decorative-edge scissors and fill with a snack mix!

Dad's Famous Steak Rub

Audrey Lett
Newark, DE

Dad loves to sprinkle this spicy mixture over steaks before grilling them...it really packs a flavorful punch. This past Christmas he sprinkled it over a standing rib roast...it was outstanding!

3/4 c. paprika
1/4 c. salt
1/4 c. pepper
1/4 c. sugar

2 T. chili powder
2 T. garlic powder
2 T. onion powder
2 t. cayenne pepper

Combine all ingredients. Store in an airtight container; attach instructions. Makes about 2 cups.

Sensational Seasoning Salt

Vickie Camp
Sulphur Springs, TX

A dear friend gave me this delicious seasoning salt recipe and I have never found a seasoning salt in the store that can compare to it. It is delicious on beef, poultry, pork, just about anything.

9 lbs. kosher salt
1 lb. pepper
6-oz. jar garlic powder
6 T. paprika

2-1/2 oz. can ground ginger
1-oz. can chili powder
1 t. dried sage
1 t. dried marjoram

Mix together all ingredients in a large airtight container. Makes about 8 quarts.

Fill whimsical retro salt & pepper shakers with salt blends and rubs...don't forget to attach a favorite recipe.

Gifts that say *Thanks!*

Kathy's Taco Mix

Kathy Otto
Blue Grass, IA

I prepare this mix ahead of time, then spoon into plastic zipping bags.
I keep several of these mixes in the cupboard for a quick & easy start
to dinner any time, and they make a perfect gift from the kitchen too!

2 t. dried, minced onion
1 t. salt
1 t. chili powder
1/2 t. red pepper flakes

1/2 t. dried, minced garlic
1/4 t. dried oregano
1/4 t. ground cumin

Combine all ingredients; divide into 4 plastic zipping bags. Use
one bag mix to one pound ground beef and one cup water. Cook on
medium heat until no longer pink; drain. Great in taco shells or taco
salad. Makes 4 bags.

Chili Seasoning Mix

Jill Carr
Carlock, IL

I make this in big batches and store it in the freezer in a jar. I have
gotten several compliments on my chili made with this seasoning mix.

2 T. chili powder
1 T. dried, minced onion
1 T. dried, minced garlic
2 t. sugar
2 t. ground cumin

2 t. dried parsley
2 t. salt
1 t. red pepper flakes
1 t. dried basil
1/4 t. pepper

Mix all ingredients together; store in an airtight container. Use
2 tablespoons per pound of ground beef for chili. Makes about
1/2 cup mix, enough for 2 to 4 batches of chili.

Harvest Loaf

Terry Christensen
Roy, UT

This delicious quick bread is the essence of autumn. I look forward to baking up a couple of batches each fall and sharing with my family & friends. This recipe was shared by a good friend of mine, I consider her to be one of the best cooks I know. I hope you enjoy this yummy bread as much as our family does.

1 c. butter, softened
2 c. sugar
4 eggs
3 c. all-purpose flour
2 t. baking soda
1 t. salt
2 t. cinnamon
1 t. nutmeg

1/2 t. ground ginger
1/2 t. ground cloves
1-1/2 c. semi-sweet chocolate
   chips
1-1/2 c. chopped pecans,
   divided
1-1/2 c. canned pumpkin

Beat butter until smooth. Add sugar; beat until fluffy. Beat in eggs, one at a time, beating well after each addition. Sift together dry ingredients; add to butter mixture alternately with pumpkin, ending with flour mixture. Stir in chocolate chips and one cup pecans. Pour into 2 greased and floured 9"x5" loaf pans. Sprinkle with remaining pecans. Bake at 350 degrees for 65 to 70 minutes. Cool for 10 minutes in pans; remove to wire rack. Glaze with Spiced Glaze while warm. Makes two loaves.

Spiced Glaze:

1 c. powdered sugar
1/4 t. cinnamon

1/4 t. nutmeg
3 T. milk

Mix ingredients together until a glaze consistency is reached.

Wrap loaves of bread in homespun napkins, bring up
the corners and tie with a big rick rack bow.

Gifts that say *Thanks!*

Sweet Potato Bread

Diane Madej
Amsterdam, NY

This recipe was shared with my 7-year-old son by his Aunt Nancy. Together they go on nature walks, visit planetariums and take science trips...this all means the world to him. My son fell in love with the flavor of this bread, and now loves to make it because Aunt Nancy shared it with him. I hope she knows how special the gift of time has been to him.

4 sweet potatoes
2-3/4 c. all-purpose flour
1 t. baking powder
1 t. baking soda
1/2 t. salt
2 t. cinnamon

1-1/4 t. ground ginger
2 c. sugar
1 c. oil
4 eggs
1 t. vanilla extract

Spray a 12-cup Bundt® pan with non-stick vegetable spray, then generously butter pan. Pierce potatoes and microwave on high setting for about 8 minutes; cool. Peel and mash. Mix together flour, baking powder, baking soda, salt and spices in a medium bowl; set aside. Transfer 2 cups mashed potatoes to a large bowl, reserving any remaining sweet potatoes for another recipe. Add sugar and oil to sweet potatoes; beat with an electric mixer on medium speed until smooth. Add eggs, 2 at a time, beating well with each addition. Add flour mixture. Beat until well blended; mix in vanilla. Bake at 325 degrees for 65 minutes. Cool bread in pan on a rack. Carefully turn bread onto a wire rack to cool completely. Makes 16 servings.

The only gift is a portion of thyself.

– Ralph Waldo Emerson

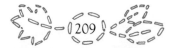

Margaret's Pantry Pancake Mix

Rita Morgan
Pueblo, CO

One wintry morning, my friend Margaret arrived at our door with a batch of this pancake mix and a bottle of real maple syrup. We invited her in, then whipped up a farmhouse breakfast...yum!

4 c. quick-cooking oats,
   uncooked
2 c. all-purpose flour
2 c. whole-wheat flour
1 c. powdered milk

2 T. cinnamon
1 T. plus 1-1/2 t. salt
3 T. baking powder
1/2 t. cream of tartar

Combine all ingredients. Divide between 4 plastic zipping bags; refrigerate. To make pancakes, beat 2 eggs in a medium bowl; gradually beat in 1/3 cup oil. Alternately beat in contents of one bag of mix and one cup water. Heat a lightly oiled griddle over medium-high heat. Pour 2 to 3 tablespoons batter onto griddle for each pancake. Cook until golden on both sides. Makes about twelve, 5-inch pancakes.

Grammy's Syrup

Virginia Scranton
Scranton, VA

This syrup is what Grammy serves with homemade pancakes...yum!

2 c. dark corn syrup
1/3 c. dark brown sugar, packed
1/2 c. water
1 c. chopped pecans

1 t. vanilla extract
4 1/2-pint canning jars and
   lids, sterilized

Combine syrup, sugar and water in a medium saucepan over medium heat. Bring to a boil; boil for one minute. Remove from heat; stir in pecans and vanilla. Spoon syrup into hot sterilized jars, leaving 1/4-inch headspace. Wipe rims; secure with lids and rings. Process in a boiling water bath for 10 minutes; set jars on a towel to cool. Check for seals. Makes about 4 jars.

Gifts that say *Thanks!*

Super Simple Scones

Robyn Goodman
Fort Hood, TX

Don't let the simplicity of this recipe fool you. These scones are super soft and scrumptious! My family enjoys them for breakfast or brunch... we've even been known to have them alongside a hearty soup or stew for lunch or dinner. You can brush with melted butter or beaten egg and then dust with sugar the last few minutes of baking, if desired.

1-1/2 c. biscuit baking mix
3/4 c. whipping cream

Optional: orange zest, chocolate chips, sweetened dried cranberries

Place biscuit mix in a medium bowl; slowly stir in cream. Turn mixture onto a floured surface. Knead in optional ingredients. Shape into an 8-inch circle 3/4-inch thick; cut into wedges. Place wedges on an ungreased baking sheet. Bake at 425 degrees for 8 to 10 minutes. Makes 8.

Fill a gathering basket with warm scones and deliver
with an assortment of flavored butters.

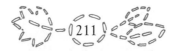

Zucchini Bread

Sharon Welch
Olathe, KS

This is one of the best recipes...it's so moist.

3 eggs, beaten
1 c. oil
2 c. sugar
2 c. zucchini, grated
1 T. vanilla extract
3 c. all-purpose flour

1/2 t. baking powder
1 t. baking soda
1 t. salt
2 t. cinnamon
Optional: 1/2 c. chopped nuts

Mix together eggs, oil, sugar and zucchini; add vanilla. In a separate large bowl, combine remaining ingredients except nuts. Add to zucchini mixture; stir in nuts, if using. Pour batter into 2 lightly greased 8"x4" loaf pans. Bake at 325 degrees for one hour. Makes 2 loaves.

Line a vintage pail with a cheery kitchen towel and tuck in freshly baked mini loaves of sweet bread...add several sample-size jars of jam too!

Gifts that say *Thanks!*

Cherry-Chocolate Chip Loaves

Vickie
Gooseberry Patch

*Try substituting sweetened dried cranberries for the cherries...
a bit tangy, but just as yummy.*

1/2 c. butter, softened
1 c. sugar
2 eggs, beaten
1 c. ripe banana, mashed
2 c. all-purpose flour

1 t. baking soda
1/4 c. chopped walnuts
1/4 c. mini semi-sweet chocolate
 chips
1/4 c. dried cherries

Blend together butter and sugar in a large bowl. Add eggs and
banana; mix well. In a separate bowl, combine flour and baking
soda; gradually add to butter mixture. Fold in nuts, chocolate chips
and cherries. Transfer to 4 greased 5-1/2"x3" loaf pans. Bake at
350 degrees for 32 to 37 minutes, until a toothpick inserted near
center comes out clean. Cool for 10 minutes before removing from
pans to wire racks. Makes 4 mini loaves.

Pair Cherry-Chocolate Chip Loaves with a tin sugar shaker...just
right for filling with powdered sugar to dust over warm slices.

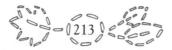

Mom's Pear Honey

Cheri Maxwell
Gulf Breeze, FL

Growing up, Dad was a beekeeper, so Mom was always looking
for new ways to use the honey. This recipe's a keeper!

4 c. pears, peeled, cored
  and sliced
1 lemon, thinly sliced
1-1/2 c. sugar
1/2 c. honey

1 T. water
Optional: 3 fresh sprigs
  rosemary
3 1/2-pint canning jars and
  lids, sterilized

Combine pears, lemon, sugar, honey and water in a saucepan over
medium heat. Bring to a boil; cook until sugar dissolves. Reduce heat
and simmer for 15 minutes, stirring often. Spoon into hot sterilized
jars, leaving 1/4-inch headspace; add one sprig rosemary to each jar,
if using. Wipe rims; secure with lids and rings. Process in a boiling
water bath for 10 minutes; set jars on a towel to cool. Check for seals.
Makes 3 jars.

Cinnamon Apple Jelly

Shelley Turner
Boise, ID

After a trip to the apple orchard, we had so many apples we spent a week
in the kitchen, but it was worth it...this jelly is just the best on biscuits.

1 qt. apple cider
2/3 c. red cinnamon candies
1-3/4 oz. pkg. powdered fruit
  pectin

5 c. sugar
6 1/2-pint canning jars and
  lids, sterilized

Combine cider, candies and pectin in a large kettle over medium heat;
bring to a full rolling boil. Add sugar; return to a full rolling boil, stirring
constantly. Boil for one minute. Remove from heat; skim off any foam.
Pour into hot sterilized jars, leaving 1/4-inch headspace. Wipe rims;
secure with lids and rings. Process in a boiling water bath for 10 minutes;
set jars on a towel to cool. Check for seals. Makes 6 jars.